D0848325

Rest

31 DAYS OF PEACE

LISA BRENNINKMEYER

www.walkingwithpurpose.com

Authored by Lisa Brenninkmeyer
Artwork by True Cotton

The recommended Bible translations for use in all
Walking with Purpose books are: The New American Bible,
which is the translation used in the United States for the
readings at Mass;
The Revised Standard Version, Catholic Edition;
and The Jerusalem Bible.

Please refer to
www.walkingwithpurpose.com
as the central location for corresponding materials and
references, and for a free printable download of
Isaiah 43:1.

20 21 22 23 24 25 / 12 11 10 9 8 7 6 5 4 3 2 1

Rest: 31 Days of Peace

ISBN: 978-1-943173-31-0

Contents

PART I
The Lover of the Imperfect

PART II
The Shepherd

PART III
How to Renew Your Mind

Dedication

To Mum~

I lift a glass of sherry to a woman I admire and deeply love, and humbly offer this little book to you. May the words in it remind you how precious you are to your heavenly Father.

Why did I dedicate this to you? Simply because I love you and you are a good woman. And you have such a strong heart. You greet each morning and search for the joy, the blessing, and the good that can be found in the simple. Countless times you could have given up or given in. But you have within you the strength of Joan of Arc, and as a result, we all have been able to stand on your shoulders.

Thank you for all the times you have said yes— to the many children God gave you, to the call to faithfulness, to long-suffering perseverance, and always, to a game of Rummikub. Thank you for sharing with me the gift of my Leo, who shares your grit, ability to smile despite sadness, and sharp wit. I'm grateful you raised him in the faith—you passed it to him, and it has held him steady.

You have built a legacy and we rise and call you blessed.

With love,

Lisa

Do Not Fear, FOR I have Redeemed YOU; I have called you by NAME: you are mine... you are PRECIOUS in my eyes and HONORED, and i love you.

Isaiah 43:1,4

The Invitation

IF YOU'VE EVER QUESTIONED WHETHER GOD truly loves you, you've come to the right place.

If you've heard Bible verses or messages about God's tenderness toward you and whispered to yourself, "That may be true for other people, but not for me," you are welcome here.

If your impression of God is as someone who is indifferent, impotent, or disapproving, you are not alone.

If you know with your head that Jesus loves you, but it doesn't feel like it in your heart, this book is for you.

I wrote this book for those of us whose hearts have been hurt, who are experiencing weariness overload, who long to feel treasured but find it hurts too much to hope. It's for those of us whose inner voice is unkind and who fall asleep at night while a litany of failures runs through our minds. It's for those who have called out for God and found Him to be silent.

The Bible is full of assurances of God's love for His people. But I know that believing those verses in theory and feeling that they are true for you personally are two different things. What I am hoping to do through this little book is close that gap.

So, I am inviting you on a journey of the soul. I know that might feel scary or like a waste of time. But what if there is more than what you are currently experiencing? What if it is possible to come to a place of inner peace where you know who you are, and you know beyond a doubt that you are seen, known, respected, and loved?

I am praying that you have just a little more hope than skepticism. That you will commit to reading a little bit of this book every day. That you will be open enough to allow a new perspective to enter your mind. That you might allow a new narrative to form as you look at the story of your life.

I believe you want to live a life of meaning and purpose. I know of no better way to help you do that than to engage your head and your heart. As you search for answers and meaning, it will always be tempting to turn to data and science to prove or disprove the various ways of looking at life and answering its biggest questions. I would encourage you to engage your head and to learn all you can, but not to rule out truths that are unseen. This is especially critical if you are trying to figure out if God exists. Would Hamlet have thought Shakespeare existed? Shakespeare couldn't be perceived or seen by him. But he was certainly there all along, writing the grand narrative.

It's also vital to engage your head and heart when you are trying to figure out what God is like. When N. T. Wright was the chaplain of the University of Oxford, he tried to meet with each new student. Many would say something like, "You won't be seeing much of me—I don't believe in God." Wright would ask them which god they didn't believe in. They'd describe the god they didn't believe in, and Wright would say, "Oh. I don't believe in that god either. I believe in the God who was revealed in Jesus of Nazareth."[1] That's where I want to begin. I'm inviting you to let Jesus' life speak for Him. This might require letting go of some ways you have thought of Him in the past.

The dendrobium orchid is a beautiful plant with an interesting trait. It has to shed its leaves in order to bloom. Those leaves have grown up with the plant, so it seems strange that they wouldn't be with it in its moment of glory. In that same way, it can feel difficult to let go of beliefs and impressions you've carried a long time, perhaps since childhood. But if we want to flourish, we have to let go of the beliefs that are not serving us well. So let's do all we can to look at Jesus with fresh eyes.

PART I

The Lover of the Imperfect

> *"If you really want to understand a man, don't just listen to what he says but watch what he does."*
>
> —*Maurice Blondel, French philosopher*

IF GOD IS LOVE, THEN WHY DOESN'T CHURCH feel like the safest place in the world? Isn't it supposed to be a haven for weary sinners? Yet a recent survey by the Barna Group revealed that a significant majority of millennials who don't go to church view Christians as judgmental (87 percent), hypocritical (85 percent), and insensitive to others (70 percent). Of those surveyed from within the Church, a lack of unconditional love was also noted, with 44 percent saying that it felt too much like an exclusive club.[2] These stats may not surprise you because of your own personal experience. Have you felt lonely in a crowd, as if no one would notice if you slipped out the door? Or have you been on the receiving end of a scornful glance, raised eyebrow, cutting words, or the message that you just don't measure up? And if you're honest, have there been times when you've been the one doing the ignoring or the judging? We are surrounded by ample evidence of mankind's difficulty in loving one another well.

All this stands in stark contrast to Jesus, who consistently chose to spend time with people whom the religious leaders shunned. But not only was Jesus drawn to notorious sinners, they were attracted to Him. Why? What was it about Him that was so appealing to imperfect people?

Let's take a closer look at the people Jesus loved in the Gospels. It wasn't just the cleaned-up, spiritually open, nicely behaved people. Jesus loved the ones with scandalous sexual sins, the perfectionists, the dirty outcasts, the cheaters, the ones who were lying to themselves, and the ones who spent most of their lives ignoring Him. Perhaps as we take a look at four women's stories, we'll catch a glimpse of ourselves.

The Unclean

A great crowd was surrounding Jesus when suddenly a ruler of the synagogue, Jairus, came and fell at His feet. A hush fell over the crowd. Everyone knew that the religious leaders were opposed to Jesus, so for one of these revered men to come and prostrate himself in front of Him would have been shocking. Jairus looked up at Jesus and begged, "My little daughter is at the point of death. Come and lay your hands on her, so that she may be made well, and live" (Mark 5:23). Jesus immediately went with him.

In that same crowd was a woman walking quickly with her head bent down. Being so close to so many people was risky. Praying that no one would recognize her, she repeated over and over again, "If I can touch even His garments, I'll be made well. If I can just touch His garments, I'll be made well." (Mark 5:28)

For twelve years, this woman had been deeply suffering from a flow of blood. Mark 5:26 reveals that she was suffering physically (doctors couldn't find a cure), financially (she'd spent all she had), and spiritually (the blood flow meant she was unclean and therefore not allowed in the temple). Not only was she too dirty to worship, all her relationships were impacted by her ailment. According to Jewish law, if you were deemed unclean, you couldn't touch anyone; your uncleanness was contagious. This meant that for twelve years, she had not been able to touch another person. She hadn't touched her children, her husband, her parents, or her friends. She experienced this shame and sense of isolation every day.

The woman came up behind Jesus, not wanting to be seen. With a heart full of faith, she reached out her hand and touched the Healer. "Immediately the hemorrhage ceased; and she felt in her body that she was healed of her disease" (Mark 5:29). In that moment, everything changed, all because of the touch of Jesus. She had placed all her hope in Him, and she was healed.

One would think that would have been the end of it—that in the press of the crowd, Jesus would have continued on to Jairus' home and the woman would have quietly moved on. Jesus had important things to do—a child was dying. And not just any child, but the child of an important, influential leader. But Jesus stopped and turned around. "Who touched me?" He said. (Mark 5:31)

"Who touched you?" the disciples asked. They looked around at the crowd and pointed out that it could have been anyone; loads of people were touching Jesus. It was a sea of humanity—who knew which hand had reached out? They needed to keep moving; there were more important things to tend to. But Jesus' eyes scanned the crowd. He looked around to see who had done it.

The woman stepped forward, trembling in fear, and fell down before Him. And in that moment, the crowd saw who she was. They saw who had touched Jesus. It was unthinkable. The audacity—to reach out as an unclean woman and touch Jesus. She would have passed her uncleanness to Him. Or so they thought.

Jesus didn't condemn her. In fact, there must have been something in His eyes, something in the way He looked at her, that made time stand still. Because the woman at his feet "told him the whole truth" (Mark 5:33). It all came spilling out—all the hurt, the rejection, the loss, the pain, the fear, the ache, the longing. She poured out her heart to Him, and He listened. He saw her. In that moment, He made sure she knew that she mattered. He said to her, "Daughter"—and this was the only time Jesus ever used that term of endearment—"Daughter, your faith has made you well; go in peace and be healed of your disease" (Mark 5:34).

What happened in that moment? Her uncleanness hadn't been passed to Jesus; instead, His wholeness and health had been passed to her. Those who were aghast that she would have had the nerve to draw close to Jesus with her uncleanness didn't understand that it was for this reason that He came.

Jesus didn't come for the healthy; He came for the sick. Jesus didn't come for the cleaned up and self-righteous; He came for the dirty and sinful. Jesus didn't come for the self-sufficient; He came for the people who needed a rescue.

These truths aren't just for the hemorrhaging woman. They are for you. *They are true for you.* In the crowd of people with all their needs, Jesus sees you. He sees the way you have suffered. He sees what was stolen from you. He sees what you have endured. He sees your grief and loss. He sees your physical pain. He sees the way people have betrayed and disappointed you. He sees the things that have caused you worry. He sees the ways you feel unworthy. He sees your loneliness.

He sees the places within you where you both long to be touched and are terrified to be exposed. He sees it all, and He cares. He doesn't look on with disinterest or impotence. He both *wants* to heal you and *can* heal you. There is healing available for your heart. He waits for you to pour out your heart to Him, to tell Him the whole truth. He will listen. He will not tune you out or interrupt you and try to fix things. He will hold space for you to release all that has been stored up and packed down in your heart.

He is reaching out to you with a hand of healing. Does that mean He promises to heal you of all the conditions in your life that you hate? That is not what the Bible promises. The healing He offers is far more powerful. He can heal your deepest brokenness—the break between you and God. That is the healing we most need, a healing of that relationship. That is the healing that stretches into eternity. That is the peace that lasts forever. And it is offered to you.

The first step to experiencing that peace is telling Jesus the whole truth. It's laying out the hurt, the mistakes, the sins, the grief, all of it. The next step is expressing your need. It's telling Jesus that you both need and want a rescue. It's admitting that you are tired of trying to save yourself, and you want *Him*. It's reaching out your hand to Jesus, just as the hemorrhaging woman did, and asking Him to make you well.

The Guilty

Throughout His time on earth, Jesus associated with the "wrong" people. He constantly invited to draw near people whom the religious leaders had deemed impure. For this reason and many others, the leaders set out to trap Him—to find an exception to the rule that would force Him to say, "Oh, you've gone too far. You don't make the cut. You aren't included. You aren't good enough." At the root of it all was their jealousy. They didn't like the way He held people's hearts and the level of influence He wielded. It was His love that was so infectious, so they did what they could to discredit Him in this very area of strength.

What was their plan? We find the answer in John 8:3: "The scribes and Pharisees brought a woman who had been caught in adultery and placed her in their midst; they said to Jesus, 'Teacher, this woman has been caught in the act of adultery. Now in the law, Moses commanded us to stone such. What do you say about her?'"

There she stood. Caught in the act. Guilty. Immersed in shame. Encircled by men ready to tear her apart. What thoughts were running through her mind? Perhaps she was kicking herself. Her own voice could have been beating her up with greater ferocity than the voices of the men surrounding her. "How could you? How stupid could you be? You're lost. You're hopeless. Now you've gone too far. There is no rescue."

What did Jesus say about her? What did He say about the woman who went looking for love in the wrong places? About the woman who had unfulfilled longings but in the attempt to satisfy them got caught in a deathlike trap? About the woman who stood there exposed, alone, guilty, immersed in shame?

"Jesus bent down and wrote with his finger on the ground. And as they continued to ask him, he stood up and said to them, 'Let him who is without sin among you be the first to throw a stone at her,' and once more he bent down and wrote with his finger on the ground. But when they heard it, they went away, one by one, beginning with the eldest, and Jesus was left alone with the woman standing before him. Jesus looked up and said to her, 'Woman, where are they? Has no one condemned you?' She said, 'No one, Lord.' And Jesus said, 'Neither do I condemn you; go, and do not sin again.'" (John 8:6–11)

Author Christopher West asks, "Why was Christ so compassionate toward sexual sinners, especially women? I think it was because, behind their deception, they were looking for him, the true Bridegroom . . . The woman caught in adultery . . . went looking for love, intimacy, and union with another; but as always, the counterfeit couldn't satisfy."[3]

What counterfeits have you tried? Have they delivered on their promises? Behind all of them is your thirst for authentic love. Jesus sees your thirst, your longing. He is waiting for you and desires to satisfy it. His love is the only one that is guaranteed to never fail you. Psalm 3:3 says, "You, O LORD, are a shield about me, my glory, and the lifter of my head." This is what Jesus did for the woman caught in adultery, and what He will do for you as well. There is an alternative to self-protection. Jesus is willing to be your shield. Can you uncross your arms and give Him access to your heart? He will not expose you. He will protect you.

Let Him uncross your arms and take your hands in His. Let Him lift your chin to look you in the eye. Listen as He tenderly whispers to you, "It's OK. Come out of hiding. You're safe here with me." He says, "There is therefore no condemnation for those who belong to Christ Jesus" (Romans 8:1). He offers you forgiveness and a fresh start.

But sometimes the difficulty lies in our ability to forgive ourselves. When this is the case, whether we realize it or not, we have set ourselves up as a higher authority than God. God has said we are forgiven. We read in 1 John 1:9, "If we confess our sin, he is faithful and just and will forgive our sins"; and in Psalm 103:12, "As far as the east is from the west, so far has he removed our transgressions from us."

When we are unwilling to forgive ourselves, we are saying that our standards are the ones that really matter. While this masks as humility, it's really pride. And this pride keeps us from approaching God for help and experiencing His love.

How did we end up here? Most of us went looking for love. And then we got burned. So we developed coping mechanisms to help us feel safe and secure. Some of us coped by keeping secrets. We tried to stay safe by building walls around our hearts. Others turned to perfectionism. Some sought comfort in food. Others sought control through eating disorders. Many of us have used alcohol to numb out and not feel things so acutely. Maybe we've shopped excessively. Perhaps we have offered our bodies in exchange for what we thought was love. The ways we've tried to cope are as varied as our suffering.

Many of these coping mechanisms started in childhood and were carried into adulthood. And then something happened: The very things that once made us feel safer and in control stopped working *for* us and started working *against* us. This means it's time to lay down those old coping mechanisms. It's time to recognize them as counterfeits. They promised safety and security, but they didn't deliver. They promised to shield us, but our hearts still got crushed.

Can you hand your coping mechanism to God and ask Him to shield you and keep you safe? There will be times when you feel uncertain, and you will be desperate to run back to your ways of trying to create safety. Could you run to Him instead?

It's time to stop holding the secrets in. God is inviting you to draw near to Him with an open and honest heart. Do not worry that you are a Pandora's box. You are not. Opening up your heart and letting God inside will not release a torrent of evil and chaos that will ruin you. You may be afraid to look at the core of who you are because every time you start to do it, you feel immersed in shame. If this happens, resist the temptation to go back to your old coping mechanisms of secrecy and hiding.

Remember, shame is Satan's tool. It's his language. It's not God's. God created us with feelings, and feelings are neither right nor wrong. They are indicators of what is going on inside us. If we didn't have them, we wouldn't know ourselves and wouldn't be able to move to a place of greater freedom. Again, when we start to recognize what we are feeling, we can begin to feel shame. We say to ourselves, "I *shouldn't* feel this way." Or "I *should* be able to just keep trucking." Shame. And then we revert to the old coping mechanisms of denial, performance, taking things into our own hands, or whatever our modus operandi has been. And all the while, God is waiting for us to come to Him and tell Him what is hurting. To tell Him how the counterfeits failed to keep their promises. To tell Him of our longing to be loved.

So share what you are feeling with Him. He can handle whatever you say. He created you with emotions. He knows that if you ignore your feelings, they will just fester and smolder below the surface. They won't go away; they will leak out somewhere else.

When you are caught in a mess of your own making, when you look at your past and are overwhelmed with regret, it may be that you can hardly bear to take a look at yourself. You might worry that being honest about who you are and what you've done will suck you into a black hole with no way out. The vulnerability appears torturous. Perhaps you assume that Jesus will speak to you in the harsh way you speak to yourself. You might think He'll judge you the way others have done. So you hide from the very One who just waits to be invited into the mess in order to restore all that seems lost and destroyed. Looking at yourself honestly is terrifying when you are alone. But you don't have to be.

Jesus stands with you when you reveal who you are and what you have done. He writes on the ground, perhaps pointing out that there isn't a single person without regrets, mistakes, and some serious failures. But those things do not make Him turn away. When you are honest and vulnerable with Him,

He looks you in the face and loves you. He tells you He understands that you were trying your best, but that sometimes your best ended up hurting you and others. He doesn't deny the mess; He doesn't say it doesn't matter. But He does say it doesn't have to have the last word. It doesn't have to define you. And if you will return His gaze, His perfect love can drive out the fear in your heart (1 John 4:18).

The Outcast

Many people sought out Jesus, calling to Him for healing and help. But for some, He went on a rescue mission. He went out of His way "to seek and to save the lost" (Luke 19:10). We find one of those stories in John 4. Let's set the scene. At this time, Israel was divided into three territories. In the north was Galilee, in the south was Judea, and Samaria was in between. Jesus was heading north from Judea to Galilee, and although the quickest way was through Samaria, that's not the route the Jewish people would typically take. There had been a feud between the Jews and the Samaritans for hundreds of years, so people would go around Samaria to avoid it. Yet in John 4:4, we read, "[Jesus] had to pass through Samaria." Why? Because He had a divine appointment with a woman at a well.

Jesus arrived at the well at noon. The sun was at its hottest, and Jesus was thirsty. It was here that

He encountered the Samaritan woman. It was an unusual time for her to come. Normally, women would go to the well to socialize and gather water in the mornings, when the temperature was cooler. But this woman came alone and at the worst time of day, precisely to avoid being seen.

Jesus approached her and asked her for a drink. She was taken aback—Jews didn't talk to Samaritans, and they certainly didn't share cups. Rabbis didn't speak to women in public; to do so would have been the end of their reputation.[4] When she hesitated, Jesus said, "If you knew the gift of God, and who it is that is saying to you, 'Give me a drink,' you would have asked him and he would have given you living water. . . . Everyone who drinks of this water will thirst again, but whoever drinks of the water that I shall give him will never thirst; the water that I shall give him will become in him a spring of water welling up to eternal life" (John 4:10, 13-14). The woman said she would love to have some of that water, and in response, Jesus told her to go get her husband and come back.

Jesus was digging into a part of her life that she'd rather He not know about, so she told Him that she didn't have a husband. "You're right," Jesus said. "For you have had five husbands, and he whom you now have is not your husband; this you said truly" (John 4:18).

What tone of voice do you think Jesus used with these words? What did His body language communicate? It must have shown compassion, or the woman wouldn't have stayed and continued talking. What do we do when we feel judged? We cover up. We try to get away. What do we do when we feel seen? We lean in.

Jesus saw the aching heart of a woman and went out of His way to bring healing. But at the same time, He was breaking down an enormous barrier between the Jews and the Samaritans. The land of Samaria had once been a part of northern Israel, but in 720 BC, the Assyrians had conquered it and deported most of the Jewish people. In their place, they brought in people from five different areas: Babylon, Cuthah, Avva, Hamath, and Sepharvaim (2 Kings 17:24). It was an effective way of subjugating a kingdom. The people eventually intermarried, which diminished their desire to rebel. To the Jewish people in southern Israel, who had not been conquered by the Assyrians, this was unforgivable. The Samaritan Jews had lost their racial purity through their intermarriage.

God had allowed His people in the north to be captured by Assyria, but He never stopped loving them and trying to bring them close again. He sent them many prophets in hopes of drawing their hearts back to Him.

As the Israelites from the north were experiencing the consequences of their sin—the loss of their nation—perhaps their thoughts went back to the words of the prophet Hosea. He had warned them that this would happen. God spoke through Hosea and said, "I led them with cords of human kindness, with ties of love; I lifted the yoke from their neck and bent down to feed them. Will they not return to Egypt and will not Assyria rule over them because they refuse to repent? . . . How can I give you up, Ephraim? How can I hand you over, Israel?" (Hosea 11:4, 5, 8).

Hosea had prophesied that "an east wind from the Lord will come, blowing in from the desert; his spring will fail and his well dry up" (Hosea 13:15). This is imagery of drought, of dryness; of lack of refreshing, sustaining water.

But God left His people with hope. In Hosea 14:4, He promised that if they would return to God, He would "heal their waywardness and love them freely"; He would be "like the dew to Israel." Healing and refreshment would come.

Fast-forward to John 4 and Jesus' divine appointment with the Samaritan woman. His meeting with her was significant in the big-picture plan of God's redeeming love, as well as in the close-up view of one woman's lonely heart. He had not forgotten the people of Israel and the promise that had been made to them. And one woman's hunger for love mattered greatly to Him.

And so as Jesus met the Samaritan woman at the well, He was fulfilling the promise that was made to the Israelites so many years ago. Jesus came to her like the dew to Israel. He offered living water to the people of the north, whose spring had failed and whose well had dried up so many years ago.

She'd had five husbands. Isn't it interesting that when the Assyrians brought in other nations, each with its own god, and settled them within Israel, there were five nations involved? Each nation had brought its own god, which had led countless Israelites to turn from God in unfaithfulness, connecting instead to the false gods.

Jesus stood before the Samaritan woman, offering restoration to her and to her nation. Yes, they had been unfaithful. Yes, they had been in a spiritually parched and dry land for hundreds of years. But living water was now being offered. God's compassion never ran out. He had come to shower her with His love and to fill her with the living water that never runs dry.

And in the heat of the day, sitting by a well, Jesus offered the Samaritan woman a glimpse into His heart. It was to her that He first shared His true identity as the Messiah. He revealed His heart and His mission to her, and in doing so, He invited her to experience the fulfillment of another of Hosea's prophecies: "And I will betroth you to me forever; I will betroth you to me in righteousness and steadfast love, and in mercy. I will betroth you to me in faithfulness; and you shall know the LORD" (Hosea 2:19–20).

Jesus was telling the Samaritan woman, "I want to be your first love. I want to be the One you run to in your hour of need." The Lord longs for that same degree of intimacy with you. How will you respond? Can you give Him a chance to talk to you without attributing to Him a tone of voice that isn't His at all?

The Perfectionist

She was just trying so hard to hold it all together. No one else saw the details she did. They thought they helped with some little gesture, but it didn't compare to the load of work she had to do. It was so aggravating to always have to ask for help—couldn't people see what she could see and just pitch in? She hated sounding needy and having to beg people to help her. But she wasn't going to throw in the towel. What would happen if she did? All the wheels would come off. It was all up to her. The weight of the world was on her shoulders, and no one understood just how hard it was for her to serve so ceaselessly. Well, she wasn't asking them to notice it all, just to do their part.

And her sister was the worst, with all her Zen-like calm, her boundaries, her priorities, her certainty that she was doing the right thing as she sat and did *nothing*. Why was no one noticing that Martha was doing *everything*? How could Jesus, who was so wise and generous, not see how imbalanced things were as Martha slaved away and her sister, Mary, sat at His feet? He must need a little reminder, a nudge, to help Him notice and simply say something.

So "Martha, burdened with much serving, came to Him and said, 'Lord, do you not care that my sister has left me by myself to do the serving? Tell her to help me.' The Lord said to her in reply, 'Martha, Martha, you are anxious and worried about many things. There is need of only one thing. Mary has chosen the better part and it will not be taken from her'" (Luke 10:40–42).

At first glance, this is not the response the hard worker wants to hear. In fact, for many Marthas, the Lord's response sounds like judgment. So let's unpack this passage while looking at what is most needed when a woman is burdened, exhausted, and perhaps even burned out.

I have mentioned the way we talk to ourselves a couple of times. This self-talk goes on and on, and we rarely note that it's made up of our own thoughts. We're more likely to attribute it to God, or to jump to the conclusion that it's what everyone around us is thinking.

Authors Emily and Amelia Nagoski refer to this voice as "the madwoman in the attic."[5] She's the mean stranger in your head who beats you up. In my head, the madwoman in the attic is the airbrushed version of me. She's at her ideal weight. She has an organized, tidy, clean, and beautifully decorated house. She's pretty, calm, cheerful, always available, and gracious. Her life is free of mess, stickiness, and tension. She highly values interpersonal harmony and fights to protect it. She might look pulled together on the outside, but underneath, she's afraid. She's afraid of having needs. She's afraid of telling the truth if it makes someone else uncomfortable. She feels responsible for others' mental well-being. She doesn't give herself permission to rest until everyone else is OK.

She stays quiet as long as the way I am behaving doesn't conflict with all that she says matters. But as soon as there is a gap, as soon as I fall short, she starts talking. "What is wrong with you? Why can't you get your act together? And don't you dare complain or ask for help, because you're the one who got yourself into this mess. And don't bother trying to talk about how you are feeling, because no one will understand. All you can do is get to work and create harmony, perfection, and beauty. Get going and fix it. You can't stop until at least the kitchen counters are wiped down. I mean, come on. That's the very minimum!"

Do you know what I feel when she starts talking? Shame. I feel immersed in it. And shame is interesting. It causes me to attribute motive. I look around and assume that everyone is judging me. These thoughts cause me to emotionally withdraw and to work at an unhealthy pace. And I don't allow myself to stop until everything is perfect.

But there is one thing that acts as a blanket over the fire of my shame, and that is empathy. When someone comes and sits with me, acknowledging what I carry and how heavy it feels without trying to fix it, my shoulders go down. My heart rate slows. I feel seen. And the shame melts away.

Let's look back at the story of Martha. When I read it, my mind jumps to Jesus' correction, when He told Martha that Mary chose better. This makes me want to close my Bible and go do something else. But I recently noticed what Jesus said first. Before He said that Mary had chosen the better part, He said, "Martha, Martha, you are anxious and worried about many things." When I am immersed in shame, I hear Him saying this dismissively, with blame and judgment. But am I not attributing a tone of voice to Jesus that isn't really characteristic of Him? Isn't it far more like Him to have said that with a tremendous amount of empathy?

What if what Jesus was doing was sitting with Martha in that gap between what is and what could be—what life was like and what she wished life was like? What if Jesus was acknowledging her fears and her worries and entering into suffering with her? Wouldn't that change everything?

What if Jesus could see that Martha was living like a performing orphan? What if He knew she was trying so hard to earn God's love, to be enough? What if He saw her tendency to equate productivity with her worth, and He knew it was killing her? What if it was with a heart teeming with compassion that He begged her to let go of the try-hard life and rest in God's love?

What if He is seeing the same things in you and is just desperate for you to experience the freedom that comes when the yoke of performance is lifted from your shoulders?

He invites you to rest. Not because all the work is done. Not because you have finally hit your quota, you've done enough, and so you now have permission to take a little break. He invites you to rest because this is your birthright as a daughter of the King of Kings. He wants you to emulate Him. Because even God rested from His labors. We see this in Hebrews 4:10–11: "Whoever enters God's rest also ceases from his labors as God did from his. Let us therefore strive to enter that rest."

When these verses tell us that we need to "cease from our labors," they're describing a faith that causes us to stop striving and depending on ourselves. It's a faith that takes self-sufficiency out at the knees and replaces it with dependence on God.

Why are we overworking? *Why* do we commit to more things than we have time for? *Why* do we get caught in the trap of perfectionism? What would it take for us to lay the burden down and rest?

When I heard theologian Tim Keller's response to that last question, it stopped me in my tracks. This is what he said: "The machinery of self-censorship must shut down in order to rest, stilling the inner murmur of self-reproach."[6]

The inner murmur of self-reproach. Do you hear that whisper?

When everything in the day quiets down, when you're lying in your bed but aren't quite asleep, does the murmur of self-reproach kick in?

Do you think about what is still undone?

Are you grateful for the elastic waist on your pajamas or the looseness of your nightgown but at the same time thinking about the weight you need to lose?

Do you dwell on the things you could have done better?

Do you regret choices you've made?

We think about all the ways we are *not* OK, the ways we are *not enough*.

We kick ourselves and determine to do better tomorrow, but then clock the hours between now and the alarm going off and think, "It'll be a miracle if I have the energy just to get up and get going." It is so hard to look at ourselves and say, "This is good" or "This is enough." It is so hard for us to reflect God after creation, look at ourselves, and say, "I am satisfied."

We can experience true rest only when we are at peace with who we are, and when who we are is uncoupled from what we do. So how can this be our lived experience? Let's go back to the book of Hebrews: "For good news came to us just as to them, but the message which they heard did not benefit them, **because it did not meet with faith in the hearers**. For we who have believed enter that rest" (Hebrews 4:2–3). The degree to which we truly believe in the Gospel determines the degree to which we can lay down our burdens and experience soul rest.

This is the good news of the Gospel:

~ It is not up to you. It does not depend on you.

~ God is not standing over you wanting you to pull yourself up by your bootstraps.

~ He is not a tyrant who is demanding that you earn your salvation.

~ He is a loving Father who was so desperate to be with you for eternity that He allowed His precious Son to be tortured and crucified so that you could be free.

You are not His workhorse. You are His beloved. Some of us believe this without a moment's hesitation.

Others believe it from time to time. Still others find it simply too good to be true.

God loves His beloved daughters far too much to leave us living like slaves when freedom is available. There is a journey He leads us on, meant entirely for our good, that helps us in this way. To be honest, a lot of the time, it really doesn't feel good.

To bring us to a place where we can understand the gospel on a deep, soul level, God allows us to go through circumstances that feel like we are being stripped. We are being taken down. We are exposed.

This process is described in Hebrews 4:12–13. I have read these verses countless times. They are very familiar to me, but I'm seeing something new in them recently. More accurately, I can say I have been experiencing these words and this process in my own life in a new way. And to be honest, it has not felt very good. Let's look at this teaching together:

"For the word of God is living and active, sharper than any two-edged sword, piercing to the division of soul and spirit, of joints and marrow, and discerning the thoughts and intentions of the heart. And before him no creature is hidden, but all are open and laid bare to the eyes of him with whom we have to do." (Hebrews 4:12–13)

The Word of God is living and active. It's not static. It's dynamic. It is moving in your life and moving in my life at the same time but in different ways. It's sharper than any two-edged sword, meaning it can go somewhere with pinpoint accuracy and hit the mark. It goes deep in our hearts and starts to reveal our motives—why we do what we do. It starts to reveal our thoughts. It starts to unearth the hurts that we have buried.

Look at how this process is described in verse 13: open, laid bare, uncovered, stripped.

This is describing spiritual nakedness that makes most of us want to hide and cover up. And isn't this what we do? As soon as God starts to really get into our business, we cover up with busyness and drivenness and restlessness.

But until we invite God into those deep places within us—until we acknowledge that we are lousy saviors and that we need healing—we will never experience rest.

When our trust in God is broken, when it's somehow fractured, self-reliance results. Self-reliance may earn us accolades as we accomplish things the world celebrates, but so quickly, it leads to sin. It leads to us putting ourselves, whether we realize it or not, into the role of God, as master of our fate. Self-reliance is the opposite of dependence on the Holy Spirit.

When God sees this, He grieves. He knows where it's coming from. He knows that something has wounded our true identity as His daughters. Saint Julian of Norwich wrote, "When God sees sin, He sees pain in us."

I think it's really important that we understand this is God's stance toward us when we are in sin. He has compassion. He sees pain in us. But because we are His precious daughters, He will never leave us in that place by saying sin doesn't matter. He will always seek to lay bare those areas of our hearts so that He can go there and bring healing to our pain.

My friend, I know how scary this is. I know the vows we make so well because I have made them myself: "I will not share my weakness." "I will be guarded." "It is not safe to be vulnerable and share honestly." I have made and lived out these vows, and do you know where this has led me? It has led me to the gerbil wheel of performance, because day in and day out, I am in the mode of self-protection.

But I am learning how to step off. I am learning to live in freedom and rest.

I have learned that when I self-protect, I cannot love. I cannot rest. I behave like a slave.

~ a slave to performance

~ a slave to others' expectations

~ a slave to perfectionism

And God holds out His hand to me, to you, and says, "Come away with Me. Come to a quiet place where all that matters is who you are in My eyes. Fix your eyes on *Me*. Lock eyes with Me.

Let the rest of the world fade away as you feel me speak over you.

I am looking at you, my precious daughter, and I am satisfied.

I am looking at you, my precious daughter, and I say you are good.

I am looking at you, my precious daughter, and I am pleased."

Why can He say this when we know all that is wrong with us, when we know we aren't perfect?

The answer is found in Hebrews 4:14–16: "We have a great high priest. He has gone up into heaven. He is Jesus, the Son of God. So let us hold firmly to what we believe. We have a high priest who can feel it when we are weak and hurting. We have a high priest who has been tempted in every way, just as we are. But He did not sin. So let us boldly approach God's throne of grace. There we will receive mercy. We will find grace to help us when we need it."

We have a merciful high priest who was radically stripped naked. Everything was laid bare when He hung on the cross. And as He died, paying the price for our sin, He cried out, "It is finished." We don't have to justify ourselves anymore. It is finished. We can walk away from our work, because we know who we are. We know what we are worth.

Jesus says, "You are worth my everything."

The Uninvited

She hadn't received an invitation to the dinner. That went without saying. Not only did she not belong, she was utterly disqualified from being in the presence of such holy people. She had sold her body in exchange for money. There was no denying it. She would never be considered suitable company. But the One she loved, a man who had seen her not as an object of pleasure, but as a person of dignity and worth, was at that banquet. So with audacious determination, she decided to show up uninvited.

The dinner was held at the home of Simon, a Pharisee and a religious leader who prided himself on his high level of adherence to the law. Jesus was reclining at the table with him when the woman stole into the room, grasping an alabaster jar filled with expensive ointment. Before anyone could stop her, she stood "behind him at his feet, weeping, [and] began to wet his feet with her tears, and wiped them with the hair of her head, and kissed his feet, and anointed them with the ointment" (Luke 7:38).

"What a scandal," Simon thought to himself. "And if Jesus really is a prophet, he would recognize what sort of a woman she is." Jesus knew. And He saw in her tears exactly what Simon needed most: a recognition of her own desperate need for a savior, and her acknowledgment of the depth of her sin. Jesus didn't see her as damaged goods; He saw her as one overcome with gratitude and love.

Jesus said to Simon, "A certain creditor had two debtors; one owed five hundred denarii, and the other fifty. When they could not pay, he forgave them both. Now which of them will love him more?" (Luke 7:41). Simon acknowledged that it would be the one who was forgiven more. Jesus continued, "'Do you see this woman? I entered your house, you gave me no water for my feet, but she has wet my feet with her tears and wiped them with her hair. You gave me no kiss, but from the time I came in she has not ceased to kiss my feet. You did not anoint my head with oil, but she has anointed my feet with ointment. Therefore, I tell you, her sins, which are many, are forgiven, for she loved much; but he who is forgiven little, loves little.' And he said to her, 'Your sins are forgiven'" (Luke 7:44–48).

The tears of the woman were the most precious offering she could give to Jesus. It was her acknowledgment of her need of a rescue. Her actions stood in stark contrast to Simon's self-satisfaction.

He kept the law scrupulously—what need did he have for a savior? The woman looked at sin as something within her, so she sought forgiveness. Simon looked at sin as something others struggled with, so he felt superior. It has always been difficult for people to grasp that "the line dividing good and evil cuts through the heart of every human being."[7]

Sin is a most unpopular word. In fact, we live in a culture that says sin doesn't exist. If we saw the woman weeping over the feet of Jesus today, we'd likely tell her that she had nothing to feel sorry for. We'd minimize her personal responsibility for her actions. We'd find something or someone to blame. We wouldn't do this out of ill intent. We'd just be trying to make her feel better, to help her to look at herself with kindness, to protect her self-esteem. But would we really be doing her a favor in minimizing her sorrow over her sin?

The philosophy of postmodernism says that absolute truth does not exist, and as a result, nor can a definitive definition of right and wrong. Any discussion of sin seems harsh and degrading to a culture that hails self-esteem as one of its core values. Most people believe that humans are intrinsically good, and that given the right social conditions, we will make the right choices. When things go wrong, we blame poverty, or dysfunctional childhoods, or sexism, or racism. I am not saying that those societal problems are not incredibly damaging and that they do not significantly contribute to what goes wrong in our world. But it's a utopian view of man that leaves all the blame there and assigns none to personal responsibility and choice.

Have you heard of Taboo? It's a game in which you are given a word, and you have to get your teammates to guess what the word is. The tricky thing is that there are five words that you aren't allowed to use, and they are the words that would make it most clear—the words that would be most helpful. Watching a person try to describe something without the needed words can be quite humorous. But it isn't so funny in real life when you're trying to answer the significant questions that people are wrestling with. Most people don't even have the vocabulary to talk about moral choices. We have taken the key words— *sin*, *repentance*, *responsibility*, *right*, and *wrong*—that would help us make sense of what is wrong with the world out of our vocabulary. That's one of the reasons we run into trouble. We are trying to explain life without being able to discuss some of the most critical concepts.

Do we not see how this results in confusion? We cannot answer the most important questions. Why am I here? Who am I? What is my purpose? How can I be happy? Could it be that in our determination to be tolerant and politically correct, we are preventing people from getting to the root of the problem, which is our need of a savior?

In Mark 2:16, some Pharisees asked the disciples why Jesus ate with tax collectors and sinners. When Jesus heard this, He said, "Those who are well have no need of a physician, but those who are sick; I came not to call the righteous, but sinners" (Mark 2:17). The sinful woman of Luke 7 recognized her profound need of God. She knew her soul was sick and needed His healing touch. Acknowledging her sin before Jesus did not reduce her to ashes; it restored her to beauty.

In the words of Father Dave Pivonka, "Jesus is loving and accepting and tolerant of every person who comes before Him, but He is not loving and accepting of sin."[8] This is not an act of anger. It's an act of mercy. Jesus sees the destructive power of sin. He sees how it distorts and disfigures love. He sees how it destroys marriages, families, and individual hearts. It creates division and confusion, and leaves destruction in its wake. Jesus hates sin because He loves us.

Jesus loved the sinful woman who wept at His feet. He didn't love her because she was aware of her sin; His love could not be increased or decreased because of anything she did or didn't do. But He loved her too much to say that her sin didn't matter. He knew it was destroying her. He knew His forgiveness would restore her.

Unconfessed sin acts as a barrier between us and God's love. This is not because God doesn't love us. It's because the wall of sin prevents us from experiencing that love. Have you ever wept over your sin? I don't ask to make you feel condemned. I ask because I know you live in the same culture I do, and overall, we tend to minimize sin. This means there is at least a chance that a part of the barrier standing between us and our experience of God's unconditional love is our tendency to forget how much we need a savior. Jesus dying for my sins on the cross doesn't really mean all that much to me if I don't think I needed forgiveness in the first place.

We read in Romans 5:8 that "God proves his love for us in that while we were still sinners Christ died for us." We will appreciate this profound display of God's love to the degree to which we understand our sinfulness. The power of the good news of the gospel can be grasped only if we understand the bad news of life apart from Christ.

Romans 3:23 reveals the dismal truth that "all have sinned and fall short of the glory of God." But it gets worse. "For the wages [consequence] of sin is death" (Romans 6:23). This is what we deserve. Whether our culture agrees with this does not make it any more or less true. In the words of Archbishop Fulton Sheen, "The truth is the truth even if no one believes it, and a lie is a lie even if everyone believes it."[9] The truth is that we all have sinned; therefore, we all deserve death. And if this were the end of the story, it would be a very sad state of affairs.

But there is more. There is good news, revealed in John 3:16: "For God so loved the world that he gave his only-begotten Son, that whoever believes in him should not perish but have eternal life." Death was the price that needed to be paid for sin. Death was the punishment—the consequence. The ones who deserve death are you and I. But Jesus stood in our place and took our punishment. On the cross, all the sins of mankind—past, present, and future— were placed on Jesus. As He hung on the cross, it was love for you that kept Him from calling down legions of angels to rescue Him. "Having loved his own who were in the world, he loved them to the end" (John 13:1). That's how He proved His love for you. He remained on the cross and gave all He had. He stretched out His arms and said, "I love you this much. To the end. Without limit."

What is the right response to so great a love? It's the willingness to have just a little more courage than fear and to come before God honestly. It's the gift of our tears of sorrow over the ways we have fallen short. It's the embracing of the gift of forgiveness. It's the offering of our hearts to the only One who can heal them.

If you feel ready, perhaps the words of this prayer can become your own:

Dear God,

I come to You as I am, aware of all the ways I fall short. Please save me. I need a rescue. Forgive me for all the times I have failed to turn to You and tried to be my own savior. Please give me a clean heart. I ask for Your Holy Spirit to fill all the emptiness in me. Help me to trust in Your unfailing love. Help me to release the grip on my own life. Take over and help me.

Amen.

PART II

The Shepherd

> *"God chose the weak of the world to shame the strong, and God chose the lowly and despised of the world, those who count for nothing, to reduce to nothing those who are something, so that no human being might boast before God."*
>
> —*1 Corinthians 1:27–29*

I CAN'T COUNT HOW MANY TIMES I'VE COME face-to-face with my genuine inadequacy. What has been needed from me, I have been unable to supply. My courage has failed me just when I needed to step up and be brave. I've had moments when I've wanted to protect my children from harm, but I couldn't be all places at all times. I've experienced too many gaps between who I want to be and who I am, and between what I need and what I have. In those moments, I didn't want to practice positive thinking and tell myself, "You're enough." I want someone bigger, stronger, more perfect than I am to swoop into my life and give me much-needed help.

I find it an enormous comfort to know that God is attracted to weakness. What do I mean by that? I mean that when I'm weak, when I recognize the enormous gap between who I am and who I long to be, God draws close and waits to see if I will call on Him. Saint Paul talks about this in 1 Corinthians 1:27–29: "God chose the weak of the world to shame the strong, and God chose the lowly and despised of the world, those who count for nothing, to reduce to nothing those who are something, so that no human being might boast before God."

Too many of us are walking around with a false, twisted idea that one has to have it all together in order to have a relationship with God. Nothing could be further from the truth. Jesus didn't say, "Come to me, all you who are cleaned up and perfect." He said, "Come to me, all you who are weary and burdened" (Matthew 11:28).

Do you know that Jesus never takes His eye off of you? He is utterly attuned to your needs. When you call out to Him, He always listens. He cannot ignore the cry of the brokenhearted when they ask for His help. One of the ways He tried to teach His disciples about this aspect of His constant care for them was by describing Himself as the Good Shepherd. We hear that phrase and picture Jesus in a long robe with flowing hair, holding a staff. The picture is nice, but it doesn't seem to have much to do with our day-to-

day experiences. But if we take a look into the way the Bible explains the role of a shepherd, we might see Jesus' care for us with fresh eyes. There's an Old Testament story that tells of a young shepherd who became a king. His name was David, and there's a lot we can learn about God from his life.

In 1 Samuel 16, God sent a prophet, Samuel, to anoint a new king of Israel. Everyone would have assumed that God would have chosen the strongest man, or the smartest one, or the most handsome. They would have thought God's choice would be someone who looked like a king. Instead, Samuel searched for the one whose heart attracted God. God had told him, "Do not judge from his appearance or from his lofty stature, because I have rejected him. God does not see as a mortal, who sees the appearance. The LORD looks into the heart" (1 Samuel 16:7).

Samuel had been sent to Jesse, the father of many sons. One after the other was paraded before Samuel, but none of them were the right choice. "Do you have any other sons?" he asked Jesse. There was one son missing—David, the youngest. He was a shepherd and out with the sheep. His father hadn't considered him important enough to present to Samuel. Samuel asked that the young shepherd be brought to him, and when David stood before the prophet, God whispered, "This is the one! This is the one who has a heart like mine. Anoint him."

David was just a shepherd, but when God looked at him, He saw a king. This wasn't because David was perfect—he went on to make some horrible mistakes, with big consequences. But God can take an enormous mess and turn it into the fulfillment of His perfect plan, and this is what He did with David. God knew that one day, the King of Kings would be one of David's descendants. He would be a shepherd king, like David, but instead of making mistakes that cost His family and kingdom their peace, Jesus would bring healing.

I can relate to David. I've made some costly mistakes, yet God has mercifully continued to work in my life to bring about His good plan. I can also relate to David's sheep on the hills of Palestine. Left to my own devices, I tend to wander and get myself into trouble. I fall down and can't get up. I eat things (literally and figuratively) that are bad for me because they are accessible and easy. I desperately need a Good Shepherd. I need a Shepherd King, one who is powerful enough to take care of me and the messes I make, who is willing to draw close to my weaknesses and protect me from myself.

The good news is that Jesus isn't the Good Shepherd only for those who stay obediently in the sheep pen. Jesus isn't the King of Kings just for the perfectly loyal subjects. Because we are God's children, Jesus promises to shepherd us and rule over our lives, messes and all. He has a message for us today from 2 Corinthians 12:9: "My grace is sufficient for you, for [my] power is made perfect in weakness." When we are weak, He is strong! We don't need to be enough, because He is all-sufficient, and He fills in the gaps when we fall short.

Does this sound too good to be true? How well we can grasp this truth—in a way that changes how we live—depends on how well we know the Good Shepherd. Who is He? Why should we trust that He is enough when we fall short?

One of the most important things to understand about our Good Shepherd is that He is a promise keeper. He does what He says He'll do. We can count on Him to fulfill those promises. We get in trouble, though, when we hold Him to promises that He never made. Nowhere in Scripture do we find a promise that says, "You'll feel happy your entire life." Or "You won't ever have to suffer." Or "You'll always be financially prosperous if you just follow me." The promises He has made, though, are the most important ones, and they are promises to provide what we truly need. Let's look at three of the promises made by our Good Shepherd. They come straight from Scripture.

He promises to lay down His life for us.

In John 10:11–13, Jesus said, "I am the good shepherd. A good shepherd lays down his life for the sheep. A hired man, who is not a shepherd and whose sheep are not his own, sees a wolf coming and leaves the sheep and runs away, and the wolf catches and scatters them. This is because he works for pay and has no concern for the sheep." Jesus rushes in when everyone else heads out the door. Regardless of what we face, nothing in our lives is too big or scary for Him.

I remember being left at home as a twelve-year-old to babysit my younger sister, Amy. I had put her to bed and was reading next door in my room. Suddenly she screamed, saying that something black was swooping around her room. I figured she just was being annoying and making it up, and I told her so. A few minutes later she screamed again, so I got up and went into her room, flicking on her lights with irritation and flinging open her closet doors while saying, "See? There's nothing!" But there was something: A huge bat came swooping out of the closet and over our heads. So I started screaming too and ran back to my bed. As it swooped up and down the hallway (no doubt panicked because it couldn't get out), Amy and I screamed in terror, afraid of it touching us or biting us or who knows what else. (For years afterward, I had to sleep with a blanket over my ear because I was afraid of something flying over my head.) And we were alone! It didn't occur to me for a second that I should fight the bat. I was the "hired hand"—just the babysitter—so I ran. As I cowered under my covers, I was desperate for my dad to get home and help us. After what seemed like an eternity, our parents came home. And this made all the difference in the world. My dad headed into the danger, Tupperware bowl and cookie sheet in hand. He battled that bat down the hallway and into their bathroom. We could hear him fighting the beast and finally catching it in the bowl and throwing it outside. What a rescue.

I knew that was how he'd respond. He loved me in such a way that I knew he'd step between me and the danger and do whatever it took to keep me safe. Our rescuer—our Good Shepherd—stepped between us and far worse danger. Instead of leaving us to fight alone, He laid down His life to protect us and lead us to a place of safety.

I realize it's easier for me to believe this than for someone whose earthly father didn't come through for them. It cannot be overstated how deeply we are impacted by the way our parents have treated us. I love nineteenth-century author George MacDonald's advice for those for whom the father image has been stained: "You must interpret the word by all that you have missed in life."[10] No one is father like God is father.[11]

Our Good Shepherd has kept—and will continue to keep—His promise to lay down His life for us. That is a promise you can stand on; it will never fail.

He promises to know and guide us.

In John 10:27, Jesus said, "My sheep hear my voice; I know them, and they follow me."

What does it mean to be known? It means that God sees into the depths of who we are. According to Jeremiah 1:5, "Before [He] formed you in the womb, [He] knew you." And Luke 12:7 tells us that He knows how many strands of hair are on each of our heads.

If ever you doubt your significance to God, read Psalm 139:

> Lord, you have probed me, you know me:
> you know when I sit and stand;
> you understand my thoughts from afar.
> You sift through my travels and my rest;
> With all my ways you are familiar.
> Even before a word is on my tongue,
> Lord, you know it all.
> Behind and before you encircle me
> And rest your hand upon me.
> Such knowledge is too wonderful for me,
> Far too lofty for me to reach. . . .
>
> You formed my inmost being;
> You knit me in my mother's womb.
> I praise you, because I am wonderfully made;
> Wonderful are your works!
> My very self you know.
> My bones are not hidden from you,

When I was being made in secret,
Fashioned in the depths of the earth.
Your eyes saw me unformed;
In your book all are written down;
My days were shaped, before one came to be.

He knows you, understands you, sees you. And He loves you.

He calls your name and invites you to come follow Him. And that's exactly what a wise sheep will do. When Jesus issues this invitation to come follow Him, He is offering the gift of guidance. This guidance is intricately tied to the promise—the truth—that He knows us.

The long periods of time that a shepherd would spend alone with his sheep helped him to know each one individually. A good shepherd would regularly check each of his sheep, looking for signs of illness and treating them with ointments as needed. Not every sheep would need the same treatment.

In that same way, our Good Shepherd looks at each one of us individually and puts together the perfect prescription to bring us safely home to heaven. He puts in a little success and a little failure, some joy and some loss, all perfectly balanced for what we need. We get into trouble when we want someone else's prescription. We all know how dangerous it is to take someone else's prescription medicine. It can be deadly. And the same is true for the prescriptions that God puts together for His children. He puts life experiences together that are the perfect combination for each of us, based on our individual needs.

He promises to sustain us and carry us when we are weak.

In Isaiah 40:11, we are promised, "Like a shepherd he feeds his flock; in his arms he gathers the lambs, carrying them in his bosom, leading the ewes with care."

Our Good Shepherd offers us comfort and satisfaction when we feel like poor, needy, weary lambs. The verse says that He gathers the lambs in His arms and carries them, then gently leads the ewes, or in other translations, "those that are with young." To most shepherds, a lamb doesn't have the same value as the mature sheep. Our Good Shepherd is different. What the rest of the world says would "fetch the lowest price in the market," God says has the greatest portion of His heart. This is a precious promise for those of us who feel weak and undervalued. Look at the care your Good Shepherd takes—He gathers you in His arms and carries you. God reiterates this promise in Ezekiel 34:16: "The lost I will search out, the strays I will bring back, the injured I will bind up, and the sick I will heal." Do you think that because of your weakness, your inadequacies, your neediness, you are forgotten? That's exactly why you are so remembered!

One of the important tasks of a shepherd is to go and look for the sheep that have wandered away and fallen down. It's essential that the shepherd finds these sheep, because if one falls on its back, there's a good chance it can't get back up. W. Phillip Keller spent years as a shepherd in East Africa, and he wrote of what he learned in his book *A Shepherd Looks at Psalm 23*. This is how he describes a sheep on its back:

> A "cast" sheep or a "cast down" sheep . . . is an old English shepherd's term for a sheep that has turned over on its back and cannot get up again by itself. A cast sheep is a very pathetic sight. Lying on its back, its feet in the air, it flays away frantically struggling to stand up, without success. Sometimes it will bleat a little for help, but generally it lies there lashing about in frightened frustration. If the owner does not arrive on the scene within a reasonably short time, the sheep will die. This is but another reason why it is so essential for a careful shepherd to look over his flock every day, counting them to see that all are able to be up and on their feet. If one or two are missing, often the first thought to flash into his mind is, *one of my sheep is cast somewhere. I must go in search and set it on its feet again.*[12]

Jesus revealed that this is His heart toward us in Luke 15 when He described the shepherd leaving the ninety-nine sheep to go in search of the one. We are not forgotten. We are precious to Him in our weakness, and when we can't pick ourselves up, He carries us in His arms.

The Sheep

In light of these revelations of who Jesus is and how He treats us in our weakness, how should we respond? We must start with a focus on the goodness of our Shepherd. When we start with us—focused on how we are supposed to behave as the sheep of His pasture—our attention tends to turn to all the reasons why we want to do things our own way. But when we take the time (daily) to meditate on the goodness of Jesus, it becomes so much easier to be who He desires us to be. We're reminded that everything He asks of us is actually for our own good.

So what should be seen in us if we are His sheep? What essential ingredient do we need to have if we're going to follow Him in paths of righteousness, if we're going to claim new ground and progress forward in the spiritual life?

A sheep that refuses to respond to its shepherd's guidance with docility continually gets itself into trouble. It's no different for us. We need to be docile and open to God's will. We can describe this in all sorts of ways—giving God the keys and letting Him be the driver of our car, trustful surrender to divine providence, submission to God's will. My favorite description is Nancy Guthrie's: "giving ourselves over to the goodness of God."[13]

When Nancy set out to practice this in her life, it was no small challenge. She had lost not one, but two children to a rare metabolic disorder, each within the first year of their lives. About a year after she lost her first daughter, Hope, she was attending a Bible study. They had been asked to read Psalm 91:1–3 and then express how it had been true in their lives: "You who dwell in the shelter of the Most High, who abide in the shade of the Almighty, say to the LORD, 'My refuge and fortress, my God in whom I trust.' He will rescue you from the fowler's snare, from the destroying plague."

As Nancy reflected on this verse, she was having a hard time seeing how this had come true. She hadn't been rescued from what she feared. The destroying plague had come, and it had taken her child. But there was something different about Nancy, which was key to her coming to a place of growth out of this incredibly painful circumstance. She wanted to grow close to God through it. She had prayed that none of her suffering would be wasted. She was seeking truth with an open heart and doing her best to give God the benefit of the doubt.

She found another passage, Psalm 59:9–11, which talked about the Israelites' enemies: "You are my strength, for you I watch; you, God, are my fortress, my loving God. May God go before me and show me my fallen foes. Slay them, God, lest they deceive my people. Shake them by your power; Lord, our shield, bring them down." Nancy started to meditate on how the Israelites were God's chosen people. Their enemies were opposed to God Himself, and He intervened countless times to protect them. The Israelites' friends were God's friends; their enemies were His enemies. He protected them out of love for them, and also for the sake of His name.

Which leads us to the question, who is the ultimate enemy? Is it the people hurting us or the circumstances we hate? Or is it neither of those things? Which enemy has God promised to protect us from?

We are promised protection, but it's protection from our ultimate enemy, sin. Because Jesus, our Good Shepherd, laid down His life for us, our ultimate enemy doesn't have power over us anymore. Sin no longer has the upper hand in our lives. It no longer has the power to entrap or destroy us. Jesus destroyed the power of sin on the cross, and now "the one who is in you is greater than the one who is in the world" (1 John 4:4).

In response to this realization, Nancy wrote, "My problem is not so much a lack of protection from

God. My more significant problem is that I'm sleeping with the enemy, justifying and enjoying my sin when all along he offers me protection from its damning power."[14]

"Our opponent [or enemy] the devil is prowling around like a roaring lion looking for [someone] to devour" (1 Peter 5:8). This is who and what God has promised to protect us from. Does this mean that we'll never suffer? No. Jesus never promised that. In fact, in Matthew 10:22, He told His disciples, "You will be hated by all because of my name . . ." and then encouraged them not to be afraid of people who want to kill them. "Do not be afraid of those who kill the body but cannot kill the soul" (Matthew 10:28).

What was Nancy Guthrie's life-changing insight from her study of these verses? She wrote, "We try to apply to our bodies His promises of protection for our souls, and we're left disappointed, accusing Him of falling down on the job."[15]

If we could truly grasp this truth, it would change the way we live. It would change the way we experience the love of our Good Shepherd. If only we would measure how much God loves us by what He did for us on the cross rather than by our circumstances.

It's incredibly hard to be docile sheep who trust the direction of the Good Shepherd and accept what He allows in our lives. It's difficult to "give ourselves over to the goodness of God." Some might even say it's impossible. And perhaps it would be, if it wasn't for the game changer, the Holy Spirit. The Holy Spirit works in our hearts, helping us to want what He wants. As we allow Him full access to our souls, our very desires are redeemed. Instead of seeing all that we'll lose if we submit to God, we see what we will gain in terms of our relationship with Him.

Instead of dwelling on what we fear will happen, we need to lay our suspiciousness of God on the table and meditate instead on His goodness. What would happen if instead of talking to friends about our doubts, we went to people who faithfully "give themselves over to the goodness of God" and asked them what that's done for their spiritual lives?

We can learn so much from the living saints around us, especially those who are willing to be shaped and changed by God in the midst of their suffering. Nancy Guthrie displayed a big view of God. Her understanding of who the Good Shepherd is changed the way she responds to tragedy. I know that the One we should always seek to imitate is Christ Himself. But I'm so inspired by women who live out their faith radically, when everyone around them gives them permission to shake their fists at God and question why. When Nancy had already lost her first daughter, Hope, and was holding her son, Taylor, who would soon die of the same metabolic disorder, she shared that a friend had asked her how she was praying for Taylor in light of what she'd been through with Hope. She told her that she found herself praying:

> "God, give us your perspective on sickness, on loss, on death, on healing." I don't want to change God's mind. His thoughts are perfect; I want to think his thoughts. I don't want to change God's timing. His timing is perfect; I want the grace to accept his timing. I don't want to change God's plan. His plan is perfect; I want to embrace his plan and see him glorified through it.[16]

I pray Nancy's example would inspire us to trust God, rather than causing us to condemn ourselves for having less faith than she displays. I pray that a vision of our Good Shepherd would so fill our minds and hearts that we'd be better able to trust in God's love, protection, goodness, and plan. He never leaves us to face our fears alone. He stands with us, and His presence makes all the difference. God's perspective and presence are the answer to the "never enough" syndrome. Never safe enough? Never good enough? Never strong enough? He is enough. He is all we need.

PART III

How to Renew Your Mind

"Be transformed by the renewal of your mind."

—*Romans 12:2*

SOME TIME AGO I HAD THE PRIVILEGE OF spending the day with a remarkable woman who has devoted her life to seeing women set free. The women who really had her heart were those who carried a weight of guilt that never seemed to lessen. These were women who hadn't known where to go or what to do, and in a pit of desperation had chosen to have an abortion. Maybe they didn't know where to turn; most definitely they were scared. Whatever their individual stories, they were now desperately longing to experience forgiveness, a fresh start, and freedom from shame.

Her time with them began with a day of prayer and healing, and the love and grace that was poured over them from religious sisters and gentle priests helped them progress toward healing and wholeness. This was followed up with a weekend retreat, offering another powerful encounter with God. Her concern was that the women, even after this point, continued to identify themselves through their sin. They weren't walking fully in freedom; in fact, they tended to return to the confessional, confessing their sin again, the same sin that God had already forgiven them for.

This didn't surprise me. No doubt, even after these deeply healing experiences, these women still heard voices in their heads that spoke words of condemnation. That told them they were damaged goods. That told them they were still dirty. That told them they weren't good enough. So they would return to the last place they heard God's voice speaking mercy—in confession.

They aren't the only women who are held in bondage by voices that condemn. Have you ever had the experience of thinking the same old deflating and debilitating thoughts, listening to the same old lies that say you are worthless, not good enough, broken beyond repair? Have you ever looked in the mirror and seen nothing but the extra pounds or wrinkles? Have you ever wanted to just give up, because the expectations scream so loud and no matter how hard you try, you know it'll never be enough?

You are not alone. Satan whispers these words to women all around the world. Do you know why? Because he is utterly terrified of what would happen if we actually believed the truth about who we are. If we saw ourselves as God sees us, if we stepped into our true identities and lived them out, if we as women called out the soul beauty in each other, we would unleash a torrent of divine love that would change the world.

But in order for this to happen, we need to cultivate our thoughts. We need to develop the habit of dwelling on God's unconditional love for us. There's much in our world that feeds us the lie that God doesn't care, doesn't exist, isn't loving, or is judgmental. Voices whisper that we are defective, are not enough, and need to be better in order to be worthy of love. We must create habits of thinking to counter all the garbage.

We have a choice when it comes to our thoughts. This means we don't need to stay stuck in cycles of thought that dwell on our inadequacies, weaknesses, and failures. It is possible to filter our thoughts through the one great truth of God's unconditional love for us. This helps us to reject the thoughts that contradict this truth, and embrace the ones that do. The third part of this book is intended to help you to do that.

We read in Romans 12:2 that we are to "be transformed by the renewing of our minds." How are our minds renewed? This happens as we learn to recognize the difference between the truth of God's Word and the lies of the enemy of our soul. So how can we tell whose voice we are hearing?

When the American Bankers Association trains tellers to recognize counterfeit money, they don't have them study fake bills. All these trainees do, hour after hour, day after day, is handle authentic currency, until they are so familiar with the genuine article that they cannot possibly be fooled by the counterfeit.

This is how we are to experience renewal of our minds. We saturate our minds with what is true—and that's found in the Bible. This is God's love letter to us. He is not silent. He speaks to us through His Word. The more we study it, the more we will recognize the voice of our loving Father.

Romans 8:1 tells us, "There is therefore no condemnation for those who are in Christ Jesus." This means the voice that condemns is not the voice of God. Condemnation is different than conviction.

The Holy Spirit *convicts* us of sin that we have not yet confessed. We feel uneasy, guilty, and God uses these feelings to draw us to confess. By contrast, the enemy of our soul *condemns* us. He focuses our attention on sin that we have already confessed and been forgiven for. Conviction and condemnation— two very different voices.

In order to help your mind recognize God's voice, I want to give you a taste of His truth each day. The third part of this book includes short readings that will daily bring your attention to how much God loves you. These are words of blessing. They should be experienced as a balm to your soul. The truths contained in the following thirty-one readings are based on the teachings of Scripture and *The Catechism of the Catholic Church*. You can trust what you are reading. It applies to you. You are not the exception to the rule.

This provides a great way to begin and end your day, by studying that day's reading in the morning and in the evening. On the first of the month, you should read Day 1. On the 15th of the month, read Day 15, and so on. When you come to the end of the month, begin again. Read this section of the book over and over again until the truths within it are a part of the way you think.

As you read, I encourage you to underline phrases that you find meaningful. Make notes of things you find hard to believe, and ask God to help you believe them. When you feel something blocked in your heart—for instance, if something you read doesn't seem like it could be true for you—pause. Ask the Lord to heal that part of your heart. You could also consider coming back to that reading each day, continuing to ask God to do a new work within you.

The repetition is the point. We need to hear things over and over to truly grasp them, especially if they touch on areas of life that have been difficult or disappointing for us.

My hope is that reading these meditations over and over will cause these truths to take root in your mind. That way when the enemy whispers lies, they won't sound right. They will conflict with things you have been reading here. I pray that the core message of *Rest*—that God loves you unconditionally and that there is nothing you can do that will make Him love you any more or any less—will root you, ground you, in God's love.

Remember, your feelings are not the boss of you. You can choose to fix your mind not on how things feel, but on things you know to be true.

Stand in the truth. God's faithful hand has held you all this way. You are still here. You are still standing. He has stayed with you this far, and He will not abandon you now.

DAY
1

"Mercy triumphs over justice."
(James 2:13)

 God the Father is completely captivated by you. He loves you. When His eyes scan the crowd and catch sight of you, He lights up with pride and says, "There's my girl."

Do you find that hard to believe? Circumstances in your past and present can make it difficult to grasp this truth, but here's the thing: Something can be true even when it doesn't feel true. Because of this, two things need to happen for us to begin understanding the heart of our heavenly Father.

First, we need to take the time to get to know God the Father better, as He has revealed Himself in Scripture. We get ourselves into trouble when we try to figure things out based simply on what we currently have in our minds and how things appear to be in the moment. The Bible is the best place to start if we are having trouble understanding who God is, because it's in His own words. It's His own witness.

Second, we need to stop judging God by our circumstances, and start judging our circumstances by a bigger view of God. All too often, we look at the things we have that we don't want and the things we want but don't have, and we conclude that God is holding out on us or doesn't care. That's what results when we judge God by our circumstances. When we develop a bigger, wider-angled view of God, we see that there is more to our circumstances, sufferings, and limitations than meets the eye. God is at work even when we don't see evidence of it.

It can be hard to believe that you have a heavenly Father who delights in you, especially if you have been basing whether this is true on how pleasant your current circumstances are. Another thing that can get in the way of opening up to the love of God the Father is awareness of all the ways you have messed up. Perhaps you look at your behavior and wonder if you're beyond the reach of God's mercy. Do you feel you've failed one time too many or that what you've done is just too awful to be forgiven? If this is the case, please hear this truth: There is no sin beyond the reach of God's mercy. Mercy always triumphs over justice.

Dear Lord,

Help me to rest with this truth on my heart: "As far as the east is from the west, so far has God removed our sin from us" [Psalm 103:12]. Amen.

DAY 2

"He found them in a wilderness, a wasteland of howling desert. He shielded them, cared for them, guarded them as the apple of his eye." (Deuteronomy 32:10)

 It's dark and frightening in the wilderness. The wasteland makes everything seem pointless and can cause us to feel ruined. When we're in the howling desert searching for an oasis, our desperation can reach a fever pitch.

This is where our Father meets us. We are lost and wandering, and He comes for us. Instead of waiting for us to clean up and make our way back to Him, He goes on a rescue mission, enters into the confusion and the mess, and grabs hold of His daughters. As we're promised in Matthew 18:14, "Your Father in heaven is not willing that any one of these little ones should be lost." That includes you. He has come to rescue you, the apple of His eye.

When we feel like God is slow to bring the relief we desire, it's tempting to assume that He is asleep on the job. But nothing could be further from the truth. According to Psalm 121, God never slumbers. He is your guardian. He's the shade at your right hand, making sure that you're not burned. Your relief finds its source in Him. He holds on to you so that your foot doesn't slip. He is guarding your soul at this very minute and forever.

Our limited perspective means that the struggle we are in the midst of isn't always what it appears to be. God has the big picture, seeing things invisible to us. Ephesians 6:12 reminds us that we aren't just wrestling with flesh and blood, but against spiritual forces. There's a spiritual battle raging around us, and God defends us in it. Although this battlefield can be invisible to the naked eye, it's no less perilous. God defends us in places where we can't even see what is truly going on.

We have an enemy who is behind all the hits we take on the spiritual battlefield. In CCC 2851, he is described as "a person, Satan, the Evil One, the angel who opposes God." When we pray, "Deliver us from evil," in the Our Father, we are not talking about evil as an abstraction. Satan is also known as the devil, and he "throws himself across God's plan."

But he is no match for God. And God is within you through the indwelling Holy Spirit. Never forget that "He who is in you is greater than he who is in the world" (1 John 4:4).

Dear Lord,

Please protect me in the wilderness.
Be my shield. Amen.

DAY 3

"The Lord is good, a stronghold
in the day of trouble; he
knows those who take refuge
in him." (Nahum 1:7)

 The first victory the enemy of our soul achieved was to convince Adam and Eve that God was *not* good, that He was holding out on them. It's the oldest trick in the book, and he continues to use it when we go through times of difficulty. Because our minds can rarely figure out how a loving God would allow our current pain, the enemy's lie seems to make sense.

When we agree with the lie that God is not good, we don't run to Him as our stronghold; instead, we rely on ourselves. We think, "God is not going to do anything about this. It is all up to me. I need to control whatever I can to minimize the damage." This determination to create control and protect ourselves does not give us the strength and support we need, and our suffering actually intensifies.

One of the hardest aspects of suffering is the sense that no one really understands what we are going through. Even when parents grieve the loss of a child, the way each experiences the grief is profoundly different. The sense of aloneness intensifies the pain. The enemy exploits this by whispering, "You are all alone. No one understands you. It's better to withdraw and try to find a solution within yourself. Don't speak. Stay silent. Isolate."

When we are suffering, it's important for us to remember that God cares. He is paying attention. When the prophet Nahum writes, "[God] knows those who take refuge in him," it means that He knows everything about us. He knows when we cry, when we pray, and when despair is overpowering our hearts. He knows our deepest desires. He knows who we want to be, and how aware we are of falling short. There isn't a groan we make, a secret longing we hold deep in our hearts, a self-deprecating thought we dwell on, a dream about to die that He does not see and understand.

He knows all about you. He has been with you in the depths of despair and on the mountaintops of joy. He knows you better than you know yourself. He can see the parts of your heart where the emotions you can't figure out dwell. You are not too complicated for Him. You make sense to Him. He asks that you run to Him for strength, comfort, safety, and protection. He offers to be your refuge and will never close the door on you.

Dear Lord,

May I see You as my stronghold, my refuge, my safe place. Amen.

DAY 4

"As far as the east is from the west, so far does he remove our transgressions from us." (Psalm 103:12)

 You are not the exception to the rule. Your sin, your failings, your shortcomings are not beyond the reach of God's mercy. Do you find this hard to believe? Are you, in this very moment, closing your heart off to the possibility that God's mercy is on offer to the likes of you? I beg you, stop. Will you just hold on to hope for one moment, and consider the possibility that you have been lied to?

Have you been told that you need to earn God's love? Have you been left with the impression that He is hard to please, and that certain sins are unforgivable? Have you believed the lie that you are damaged goods, beyond repair? How this grieves the heart of the Father. People put words in God's mouth that He never said. He is poorly represented constantly. Can we give God the floor and allow Him to speak for Himself?

Satan whispers the lie that you aren't good enough, that God could never love that part of you. But the truth is found in Romans 8:38–39: "Neither death nor life, neither angels nor demons, neither the present nor the future, nor any power, neither height nor depth, nor anything else in all creation, will be able to separate us from the love of God that is in Christ Jesus our Lord."

Satan whispers that the sin you are struggling with is beyond the reach of God's forgiveness. But the truth is found in 1 John 1:9: "If we confess our sins, he is faithful and just and will forgive us our sins and purify us from all unrighteousness."

Satan whispers that we'll never change. We're damaged goods. Satan whispers that we'll never get away from that past sin . . . it's a part of us . . . stuck to us like tar. But the truth is found in 2 Corinthians 5:17: "If anyone is in Christ, he is a new creation, the old has gone, the new has come."

We are not who we used to be. We are no longer defined by how we've been treated or choices we've made. We get a fresh start. When we are forgiven, we are washed clean. No exceptions.

Dear Lord,

Your mercy seems too good to be true. I'm so afraid to open my heart to the possibility that Your love is unconditional and Your forgiveness is without measure. So help me to trust. Help me to have just a little more courage than fear to open my heart to You and Your mercy. Amen.

DAY 5

"For God so loved the world that he gave his only-begotten Son, that whoever believes in him should not perish but have eternal life." (John 3:16)

This is one of the most beloved verses of the Bible, and for good reason. It summarizes the extent of God's love and reveals who is the recipient of it. Who is the object of God's love, revealed in John 3:16? It's the world. This was a radical thought for the religious people of Jesus' day. They knew that God loved, but they assumed His love was reserved for the Jewish people. To hear that God loved everyone was new and scandalous to many. God loves His own—His people—but His love extends beyond. He loves the world and all who are in it. The arms of God are wide enough to embrace all of mankind.

This is what *The Catechism of the Catholic Church* says about the intensity of God's love:

> God's love for Israel is compared to a father's love for his son. His love for his people is stronger than a mother's for her children. God loves his people more than a bridegroom his beloved; his love will be victorious over even the worst infidelities and will extend to his most precious gift: "God so loved the world that he gave his only Son." (CCC 219)

Do you have secret sins that you are certain disqualify you from receiving God's love? This bears repeating: God's love "will be victorious over even the worst infidelities." There is nothing beyond the reach of God's love. His mercy is always enough to cover and cleanse us from every single sin. There is nothing He will not forgive, if we but ask.

God loves the entire world, but the entire world does not receive all that He offers. His offer is dependent upon *each person* choosing to receive it. Whether we reject it because we feel unworthy or because we don't think we need it results in the same end: We don't receive the gift. And what is the gift? It's Jesus Himself, and the divine life that He brings. It's the promise of eternal life. It's an offer to all, but we must choose to receive it.

If someone gives you a gift but you leave it unopened on the shelf, have you truly received it? No. In that same way, God's gift of love, forgiveness, and eternal life is offered to you, but you need to open your hands and heart and accept it.

Dear Lord,

Please forgive me for underestimating the breadth and depth of Your love. I want to receive the gift of Jesus' presence. Amen.

DAY 6

"He brought me to the banqueting house, and his banner over me was love." (Song of Solomon 2:4)

 What is the purpose of a banner? It's a flag or a standard, raised during a battle to indicate the rallying point. This is where the eye is supposed to go, and the symbol on the banner is to remind the warriors what they are fighting for. Picture exhausted soldiers in a grueling battle, and then a white stallion breaking through the ranks, one brave mounted soldier waving their country's flag, calling them to be brave and fight for what they love. It lifts eyes to the purpose of the battle and offers hope.

The banner God raises above us is a banner of love. It was for love of you that Jesus sacrificed His life. It was for love of you that God brought you into the world. It was for love of you that God created beautiful sunsets, majestic mountains, and the raging sea. It was for love of you that God allows both the hard things and the delightful ones to intersect your life. He looks at you and the overwhelming emotion felt is love. Raise your eyes to the banner of love.

The banqueting table He invites you to is both now and later. One day you'll be invited to the heavenly banquet, where the feasting will be beyond compare. That will occur later, but now He invites you to the banqueting table of this life—this one wild, unpredictable life that while containing heartache, also brings moments of pure joy, surprise, and beauty.

A battle rages every day in that space between you and that banqueting table. The enemy wants to keep you from sitting down and enjoying the life God has prepared for you. He wants your focus to remain on all the things you don't like and to prevent you from practicing gratitude. Gratitude clears a path straight to the banqueting table. The enemy wants to keep your focus down, not up. If you look up, you'll see the banner of love waving above your head, and it will change your perspective. It'll rally you to move toward the banqueting table.

Keep your eye on the banner. Remember, everything that happens to you has been filtered through the Father's love. It can all be worked for good in His capable and tender hands. Look for the blessings. Keep an eye out for the surprises God has placed in your path today—the little consolations, the small things that can deliver great joy if you slow down and really see them.

Dear Lord,

Thank You for inviting me to the banquet of my unique, handpicked-by-You life. I raise my eyes to the banner of Your love and pray that they remain there throughout my day. Amen.

DAY 7

"He saved us, not because of deeds done by us in righteousness, but in virtue of his own mercy, by the washing of regeneration and renewal in the Holy Spirit, which he poured out upon us richly through Jesus Christ our Savior." (Titus 3:5–6)

 So many of us head into each day hoping that our performance will earn us the verdict of "good enough." Every morning we are, in essence, getting ready for the trial we think we're going to face. In this tribunal, we have to prove that we are enough—young enough, smart enough, good-looking enough, successful enough, holy enough, thin enough. Some days we feel we've nailed it. Other days we don't. A new day dawns, and the proving just starts all over again. We never quite get to that place where we can say, "Done." The result of this yo-yo life? Insecurity and exhaustion.

But a game-changing event took place more than two thousand years ago, and it changed everything about this tribunal. When we forget this, when we relegate this fact to a part of our lives reserved for Sunday, we miss out on the peace we are promised.

What happened when Jesus died on the cross all those years ago? He entered the courtroom on our behalf. He stood trial for all our sins and shortcomings. When the guilty verdict came in for what we had done, Jesus took the punishment in our place. What did He say on the cross just before He died? "It is finished" (John 19:30).

So when we choose to go into the courtroom each morning, ready to be on trial for our worthiness, God waits for us to turn and notice that He is there, and He has something to say to us. Sometimes we rush by Him because we're so busy with so much to prove. But when we take the time to pause, when we turn our face to His, He tells us, "You don't have to go in there. The trial is over. The punishment has already been meted out and was paid for by me. You are free to go and live differently."

There is nothing to prove when we know that we are forgiven.

There is nothing to prove when we know that we are unconditionally loved.

There is nothing to prove when we know that we are accepted by God, not because of anything we have done, but because of what Jesus has done.

It's already been decided. The jury is in. You have been declared enough, not because of any righteous things you have done, but because of Jesus and what He did.

Dear Lord,

May I pass by that courtroom door each day and instead come into Your presence. Amen.

DAY 8

"Forgetting what lies behind and straining forward to what lies ahead, I press on toward the goal for the prize of the upward call of God in Christ Jesus." (Philippians 3:13)

 Are you dragging unnecessary baggage along on life's journey?

Some of us are carrying the good girl's suitcase. We figured out early on what the expectations were, and we set out to meet them. We've been good girls for so long, it's second nature. Reputation is important, so we work to keep ours impeccable. We hide behind masks because being weak, being afraid, and being a mess affect what people think of us. We follow the rules. We serve where needed. We hear that the Christian life is supposed to be about freedom, but to us, it just feels like hard work. Sometimes we get a little frustrated with a God who expects so much. We look at pursuing lasting purpose according to God's design and wonder if this means we'll just have a whole new area where we need to perform. That's a heavy suitcase to drag around.

Some of us are dragging the suitcase of guilt. It's filled with past sins—some confessed, some not. All together, they weigh a ton. When Christ invites us to seek forgiveness, we peek inside and conclude that this garbage is just too much. It's too wretched to bring to the surface. Even if God might forgive it, we say that we can't forgive ourselves. We ignore the pride implicit in setting ourselves up as higher judges than God and keep lugging this junk on the journey.

Some of us are holding tight to the suitcase of bitterness. Too many dreams have been dashed. We've believed in promises in the past, but their fulfillment has been too long in coming. We've resigned ourselves to just getting through life. Why hope if we're just going to be disappointed? This suitcase is sitting on our hearts and weighing us down. We feel the continual heaviness, and there seems to be no relief.

Jesus wants us to drag all these suitcases to the foot of the cross and leave them there. He wants to take our encumbrance of past mistakes and exchange them for His forgiveness. He invites us to take our burden of perfectionism and attempts to earn God's favor, and exchange it for His unconditional love. He longs for us to bring our bitterness to the cross and look up to see our champion, who will fight for us and right every wrong.

Dear Lord,

I want to answer the call to forget what lies behind and strain forward to what lies ahead. Eyes up, forward focus! Amen.

DAY 9

"Greater love has no man than this, that a man lay down his life for his friends." (John 15:13)

 We question a person's faithfulness to us when we sense that his or her motive in the relationship is self-seeking. When we recognize that someone is really out for him- or herself, we know that a time may come when we end up hurt or betrayed. This is why it's so important for us to recognize that God's desire for us is utterly pure. He is not self-seeking. He has proven on the cross that His love for us is selfless. "For God so loved the world that he gave his only-begotten Son, that whoever believes in him should not perish but have eternal life" (John 3:16).

Father John Bartunek reflects on this in his book *The Better Part*:

> No hidden agenda, no selfish undertones—pure generosity. This is the heart of God, of the Lord who longs for our friendship. Only when a Christian internalizes this fundamental and overarching motive of God does Christian discipleship really begin to mature. This is Christ's revolution. That disinterested, self-forgetful love has the power to overcome all evil and renew

every human heart and the human race as a whole.[17]

Something you can count on: God is *for you*. When important people in our lives fail to love us well, we often allow those experiences to cloud our impression of who God is and how He loves us. The truth is, God's love is perfect, never failing, and ever enduring. Oh, that we would have grace-healed eyes that can see Him as He is.

Dear Lord,

You have proven Your faithfulness to me on the cross. Thank You for resisting the urge to call down legions of angels to rescue You. Thank You for staying there until my freedom was won. Amen.

DAY 10

"For you did not receive the spirit of slavery to fall back into fear, but you have received the spirit of sonship. When we cry, 'Abba! Father!' it is the Spirit himself bearing witness with our spirit that we are children of God." (Romans 8:15–16)

Sometimes we look at Christianity as the way to make sure that we are forgiven. We're covering our bases so that we are "safe" (as in baseball). But when we stop there and go no further, we totally miss out on what God (and Christianity) really offers. What God is truly after is so much more than just forgiving us. He *wants* us. He longs for us to come home to Him, our heavenly Father. Christianity is all about relationship.

When we read the story of the prodigal son, we can mistakenly think it's all about the son finally coming to his senses and asking for forgiveness. But the real focus of the story is the father's heart. It's the picture of the father running to his son the minute he sees him on the horizon. It's about the compassion and joy and mercy that the father is completely thrilled to pour all over his child. And that is exactly how God the Father feels about you.

You are the daughter of a strong, faithful, totally engaged Father, a Father who loves you too much to ignore self-destructive sin in your life, a Father who made sure you had a safe way to get home to Him even before you were born, through Christ's death and resurrection.

Your Father is going to go the distance with you. He knows that you need Him for the long haul. You need to be able to count on Him to stay when everyone else leaves. You'll never stop needing His direction, guidance, and parenting. And that's OK, because His love for you is never-ending. His arms are always open. You are His beloved. You are safe with Him.

Dear Lord,

I don't want to run anymore. I want to come home and rest. Thank You for always keeping the door open. Here I am, Lord. Here's my heart. Amen.

DAY 11

"The Lord, your God, is in your midst, a warrior who gives victory; he will rejoice over you with gladness, he will renew you in his love; he will exult over you with loud singing." (Zephaniah 3:17)

You are delightful to God. Everything about you—the quirky things, your talents, your weaknesses, your physical features, your emotions, He loves it all. He is drawn to you with the purest of love and motive. Each morning, He is there, wanting you to turn to Him for a pep talk. He knows what you're going to face today and exactly what you need in order to go forward with strength and grace. When you rush out the door, too busy to spend time with Him, He waits. You are always on His mind. He sings over you throughout the day because you are such a source of joy in His life, and because He hopes that you'll hear a strain of the music and turn your face to His.

God is a warrior who is always fighting on your behalf. He is aware of the enemy's schemes. Before they even occur, God has ordered it all to your good. He is stealthy, tireless, strong, strategic, courageous, and decisive. Nothing surprises Him.

When you are weary, God knows what will deeply satisfy and replenish you. You often turn to other things when you are worn out, and while there's nothing wrong with watching Netflix, it doesn't ever renew you deep down, and it's deep within that you are weary. God can go there and do unseen work that rebuilds and strengthens you on the soul level.

What might really refresh you is honest confession. Cleaning out the junk in your heart will leave you feeling free and light. People resist what is best for them, so it's critical to build confession into life as a habit, something done without even thinking about it. When you are weary, you are usually far more aware of what others are doing to frustrate you than what you are doing to make things worse than they need to be. Owning your part of the problem, searching for ill motive, and recognizing when you have fallen into pride, just to name a few steps, can set you on the road to consolation.

Dear Lord,

Thank You for seeing the obstacles in my life, every single one of them, and fighting for me. May I listen for the faint strains of Your singing in my day; it comes in the moments that delight me. May I recognize that all those fragments of joy were sent to me by You. Amen.

DAY 12

 What has been flying at you lately? Harsh words? Too many tasks? Financial demands? Heartache? Disappointment? Perhaps what has come your way has been good, but too many opportunities have left you unsure of what you should do next. When you feel as if things are coming at you and you are reacting instead of responding, you need something to shield you from it all.

God is your shield. He stands between you and the tasks, needs, heartache, disappointment, and opportunities and says, "Slow down. Hit pause. Breathe." He holds it all back and asks you to look Him in the eye. He reminds you that He has got everything under control. Knowing how overwhelming it can be, He helps you to see what the next right thing is. The whole plan won't be handed to you; He wants you to come to Him continually. But He'll shine light on the next step.

When it's words that have hurt you, He stands as a shield between you and the opinions of others, reminding you that His opinion is the only one that ultimately matters. He is a balm on the wounds of your heart. He is your defender and guardian.

But God offers more than protection. He lifts your head and offers you hope, which comes when you gain a perspective that is higher than your circumstances. There may be nothing glorious about what is going on in your life, but there is glory in God. When you focus on Him—when you live for an audience of one—you can let other things fade into the background.

We can find glory in a lot of things—power, reputation, achievements, possessions—but none of those things give us lasting satisfaction. In fact, the more we have of each of these things, the more we want. True contentment never comes from getting the next thing on the list, because it is always replaced with a new longing. Our desire for just a little bit more will never be satisfied if we are seeking glory in the wrong things.

Needs around us will be never-ending. The only way we will avoid all this need is by isolating ourselves from others, and that is a poor solution, as connection and community are necessary for happiness. But God shields us from all of it and allows us space to think, prioritize, fix our eyes on Him, and go forward.

Dear Lord,

Thank You for being my shield. Please lift my head so my eyes remain on You. Amen.

DAY 13

"How great is the love the Father
has lavished on us that we should be
called children of God!" (1 John 3:1)

 You are the daughter of a generous,
protective, and engaged Father, a
Father who will never leave you or
abandon you.

And for many of us, this is one of the hardest things
in the world to truly believe.

In Matthew 7:9–10, Jesus asked, "Which one of you
would hand his son a stone when he asks for a loaf of
bread, or a snake when he asks for a fish? If you then,
who are wicked, know how to give good gifts to your
children, how much more will your heavenly Father
give good things to those who ask him." If imperfect
earthly fathers (at least ones who aren't cruel or
somehow unable) give their children what they need,
we can count on our heavenly Father to give us good
things, as opposed to holding out on us, if we ask Him.

The seed of doubt regarding the Father's goodness was
planted in the Garden of Eden. God had surrounded
Adam and Eve with beauty, abundance, and provision.
Only one thing was withheld, the fruit from the tree of
the knowledge of good and evil. The serpent slithered
up to Eve and asked her, "Did God really say, 'You

shall not eat from any of the trees in the garden'?" (Genesis 3:1). Look at him, making God's restriction sound worse than it actually was. See how the liar exaggerated in order to make his point? And Eve paused and engaged with the enemy. She leaned in and listened to the father of lies (John 8:44) and added to God's words. Instead of saying only that they weren't to eat the fruit, she said that they weren't to touch it either. The truth about God's words became fuzzy, and the slide toward compromise and slavery to sin began.

Are you done listening to lies? Are you ready to take a leap of faith, a step toward believing that God the Father loves you and is treating you as a good father should?

Dear Lord,

I'm done listening to lies. I may not understand why You have allowed certain things into my life and withheld others, but one thing I do know: I want my mind to be filled with truth. So I ask You, Jesus, what is the lie that I am believing about the Father? [Pause, and pay attention to what comes to mind. Then take the first lie that comes into your mind.] Jesus, will You take that lie from me forever? Father, what's the truth? Show me who You really are. Amen.

DAY 14

"A bruised reed he will not break,
and a faintly burning wick he
will not quench." (Isaiah 42:3)

So many of us have an image of God as one who sets a high standard and gets disappointed and perhaps angry when we don't meet it. Is this really who God is? I don't believe so. God knows our limitations. He is very familiar with our weaknesses. While people in our lives may have unrealistic expectations of us, God sees the whole picture and the degree to which we are trying. And when we're weary, He comes to us with arms of comfort, eyes of understanding, and lips that speak encouragement. When we are weakest, He asks us to rest in His lap and lay our head on His strong shoulder. He doesn't want to break us; He came to restore us.

This is the heart of the Gospel. God saw the chasm that sin created between us and Him. He knew that no matter how hard we tried, we'd never be able to achieve the perfection required to be in His presence. Instead of telling us to jump higher or try harder, He stooped down and said, "I'll do for you what you can't do for yourself." Jesus, who had never sinned, allowed all the sins ever committed to be placed on His shoulders. He paid the price of sin so that we wouldn't have to.

Jesus' sacrifice cleared the way so we could have a personal relationship with God. This is a privilege offered to everyone but enjoyed by relatively few people. Do you know *about* Jesus, or do you know Him personally? I don't ask this question as a rebuke, but rather as an invitation. He's inviting you to draw closer.

Once we know Jesus personally, we never need to be lonely again. We no longer have to worry about being perceived as too emotional when we pour out our hearts. We don't have to worry that our private concerns will be gossiped about if we share them with Him. He is the most intimate, true friend, connecting with us body, soul, and spirit.

Because of Jesus, we can let go of the try-hard life. We can rest in His all-sufficiency. We can ask the Holy Spirit to run through us like sap through a tree, nourishing us and doing in and through us what we can't do for ourselves.

Dear Lord,

What I have the least of is _____
(patience? love? empathy? strength?).
I am storming heaven with my prayer,
asking You to give me what I lack.
Help me today, Lord. Amen.

DAY 15

"It is no longer because of your words that we believe, for we have heard for ourselves, and we know that this is indeed the Savior of the world." (John 4:42)

These words were spoken by the Samaritan people after they had heard the testimony of the Samaritan woman at the well. She had convinced them to come and listen to Jesus, and their belief was the result of that personal encounter with Him.

Many of us believe because of other people's words. We hear the priest talk about Jesus on Sunday, we've heard Christian authors talk about their relationships with Christ, we've listened to some podcasts and gained spiritual insights. All these things are good, but they are nothing compared to hearing for ourselves. By this, I mean having a direct encounter with Jesus Christ.

"That's not for me," you may be thinking. "That's something reserved for a special group of people." If these are your thoughts, I want to gently protest. Because nothing could be further from the truth.

Jesus wants to encounter you personally. If you were the only person on earth, He still would have come and died on the cross for you. He doesn't look at mankind as a group of indistinguishable people.

He is able to see each person, individually. In Luke 12:7, Jesus said, "even the hairs of your head are all numbered." He knows you, better than you know yourself. He can see into the depths of your soul.

This truth can make some of us want to cover up the parts of us that we think must be repugnant to Him. When we do, His heart is grieved. What Jesus deeply desires is for us to invite Him into the mess and ask Him to clean it up. He doesn't find our weakness revolting. He finds it inviting.

How do we encounter Jesus? Through prayer. You can go to a church, spend time in adoration, or stay home. God will meet you wherever you are. The words don't need to be fancy, just heartfelt. You might want to place your hands on your thighs, palms up, as a gesture of surrender.

Dear Lord,

I want to encounter You personally. I open my heart to You and ask You to come in. Please reveal Yourself to me. Amen.

DAY 16

"Take my yoke upon you and learn from me; for I am gentle and lowly in heart, and you will find rest for your souls." (Matthew 11:29)

The word *yoke* comes from the Greek word *zugos*, which can also be translated as a pair of scales. It's as if Jesus is saying, "Take off your old yoke. It represents a way of weighing what's most important, and it's a broken scale. Replace it with my yoke. Replace it with my pair of scales. You'll find rest when you measure things as I do. What I consider most important each day isn't burdensome."

There are times when our expectations for ourselves are in areas that are not important to God. Failure in those areas gives us an opportunity to evaluate what matters most—perhaps those expectations weren't worth pursuing in the first place. Sometimes we have expectations in areas that God does care about. For instance, He wants us to grow in intimacy with Him and in holiness. It isn't wrong for us to have expectations and hopes in the area of spiritual growth.

The problem isn't always the expectation itself. Often, it's how we react when we fail. Do we wallow in self-pity? Do we quit? Do we turn to escapism? God wants us to get back up and persevere on our journey of spiritual growth.

It's very hard to let go of our expectations when we continue to measure our worth with a faulty scale. If our worth is tied to what we achieve, then the drive to be acceptable, good enough, or extraordinary will kick into gear, impacting our actions and attitudes. Good days will be ones when we meet all our expectations. They will be rare.

Grace-healed eyes look at life differently. They recognize that our worth was measured in one place, on the cross. When Jesus died in our place, He declared us worth everything. Our worth isn't tied to what we do. It's tied to whose we are. We are God's beloved daughters. Toss out the old scales. They are only making you miserable.

Make a list of some of the things you are expecting of yourself right now. Are any of those expectations unrealistic during this season of life? Circle the expectations that you believe matter to God. To help you discern this, ask yourself, "If I don't meet this expectation, will Christ be upset?"

Dear Lord,

May Your grace do its healing work in me.
I am resting in Your arms, closing my eyes,
and just sitting in Your presence. Amen.

DAY 17

"Therefore do not be anxious about tomorrow, for tomorrow will be anxious for itself. Let the day's own trouble be sufficient for the day." (Matthew 6:34)

 Anxiety grips our emotions, harms our health, and leads our thoughts down a path that culminates in fear. Often we feel we can't get out from under our anxious thoughts, which take on a life of their own as we imagine worst-case scenarios. These thoughts omit God from the picture. In the words of author Linda Dillow, "Anxiety is that which divides and distracts the soul, that which diverts us from present duty to weary calculations of how to meet conditions that may never arrive. It's the habit of crossing bridges before we reach them."[18]

God goes ahead of us. In His timelessness, He is already in our tomorrows. There is nothing we will face that He has not evaluated before He allows it to touch us. And He promises that He'll never allow us to face things that are beyond our ability to bear, provided we lean on Him for grace.

When an anxious thought comes into our minds, we have a choice regarding how we will respond. Will we play with it? Will we travel with it into the future in our imaginations? Or will we stop that thought in its tracks, grab hold of it, and offer it to Christ? This is what is meant by 2 Corinthians 10:5: "Take every thought captive to obey Christ." We take it captive by replacing the worry with a truth that builds our trust in God.

Read the following words from the devotional *Jesus Calling* as if they were Jesus' words to you:

> Anxiety is the result of envisioning the future without Me. So the best defense against worry is staying in communication with Me. When you turn your thoughts toward Me, you can think much more positively. Remember to listen, as well as to speak, making your thoughts a dialogue with Me.
>
> If you must consider upcoming events, follow these rules: 1) Do not linger in the future, because anxieties sprout like mushrooms when you wander there. 2) Remember the promise of My continual Presence, include Me in any imagery that comes to mind. This mental discipline does not come easily, because you are accustomed to being a god of your fantasies. However, the reality of My Presence with you, now and forevermore, outshines any fantasy you could ever imagine.[19]

Dear Lord,

Help me to discipline my mind to stay in the present moment. But when I need to think about the future, may I always do so with a picture of You in the midst of anything I might face. Amen.

DAY
18

"I have loved you with an everlasting love; therefore I have continued my faithfulness to you." (Jeremiah 31:3)

How do you measure your worth? No matter where you go, you are continually receiving messages about what our culture says matters most. Airbrushed images of models cause you to make outward beauty the measure. Pinterest and glossy magazines tempt you to measure your worth by the perfection of your home. The achievement-oriented culture tells you that your worth is measured by your accomplishments.

The checklist is long: Have a perfect body, perfect health, perfect clothes, be a perfect mother, have a perfect marriage, achieve a perfect career, and consistently give back to those less fortunate. The result? Pressure, and a nagging sense that no matter what, you'll never be enough.

Author Richard Winter describes the consequence of living under this pressure:

> The core of the problem is that when a person's self-worth depends on reaching those high standards, it is an inevitable script for self-defeat and their own personal hell of repeated failure and eternal regret.[20]

If you wonder if your self-image is tied to these standards and measures, ask yourself the following:

~Does my sense of worth change when I'm fifteen pounds overweight?

~Does my sense of worth fluctuate depending on what I've accomplished in a day?

~Would my sense of worth change if I had to downsize or scale back because of financial difficulties?

God wants you to be freed from these faulty measures of your worth. He already measured your worth when Jesus hung on the cross, and He declared you worth dying for. He loves you and wants you to be rooted in that unconditional love. Perhaps you were loved conditionally in the past. God's love is different. Receiving and soaking up His unconditional love is the antidote to the bondage of trying to measure up to the perfect standard that the world says matters.

Sometimes it's hard to believe that you are treasured and loved by God. But you have to decide—whose voice are you going to listen to? Whom will you believe?

Dear Lord,

Your love for me is everlasting. It is unconditional and doesn't fluctuate depending on what I accomplish in any area of my life. Even "spiritual achievements" don't cause You to love me more or less. May I let go of the try-hard life, which ends in defeat and heaviness of heart. Instead, may I be rooted and grounded in Your faithful love. Amen.

DAY
19

"And I will put my spirit within you, and cause you to walk in my statutes and be careful to observe my ordinances." (Ezekiel 36:27)

How is the human heart changed from a heart of stone to a heart of flesh? God puts His own Spirit, the Holy Spirit, within us. The Holy Spirit, the third person of the Trinity, is the love between God the Father and Jesus the Son.

There are so many times in our lives when we whisper, "I can't." I can't be more patient with my kids. I can't forgive him. I can't keep going. I can't bear this loss. I can't give any more.

The Holy Spirit comes to us in those moments and whispers:

I know you can't. I see. I see your limitations. I see your hurts. I see what's been done to you. But even though you can't, I can. I have come to break all the chains that keep you from living the life of freedom that you were meant to live. You were made for more, daughter of God. I am here for you. I am for you. My love for you is relentless.

I am your **Comforter** (one who relieves another of distress).

I am your **Counselor** (one whose profession it is to give advice and manage causes).

I am your **Helper** (one who furnishes another with relief or support).

I am your **Intercessor** (one who acts between parties to reconcile differences).

I am your **Strengthener** (one who causes you to grow, become stronger, endure, and resist attacks).

Is there a place in your life where you are not living in freedom? Do you feel chained to old habits of behavior and powerless to change? Do you feel bound by lies about your identity—lies that say you are worthless, or ugly, or stupid? Do you feel stuck in the rat race, unable to slow down, unable to breathe? These are the very places where you need to invite me to come and set you free. Don't treat me as an interesting character in a book. Ask me to jump off the pages of the Bible and into your heart.

Dear Lord,

Breathe on me, breath of God. Come, Holy Spirit. Come. Amen.

DAY 20

"[May] the eyes of your heart [be] enlightened, that you may know what is the hope to which he has called you." (Ephesians 1:18)

 When we experience distance in our relationship with God, it is not because He has moved away from us. It's because we hide in fear, hang our heads in shame, or stick up our noses in pride. We'll do anything to avoid making eye contact with God. It reminds me of times my kids have done something wrong and I'm trying to discipline them. Sometimes they respond with their arms folded, staring at the floor in anger. They are mad that they've been caught. Other times their face is in their hands, and they can't stop crying because they are so upset over messing up. No matter what the heart attitude, what I really want them to do is look me in the eye. I want this for two reasons. One is for them to know that I'm serious about what I'm saying. But I also want them to see the unconditional love in my eyes.

When God invites us to the sacrament of penance, He's asking us to look Him in the eye. He wants to make eye contact with us. In that moment, we can see ourselves from His perspective. Yes, our sin is serious. He isn't saying it doesn't matter. But it doesn't diminish His love for us. In the confessional, we look the Lord in the eye and experience a moment of deep tenderness as God whispers, "It's OK. You're safe here with me. You can stop hiding."

The Lord is inviting you to come and gaze into His eyes of mercy. He's offering you hope for a fresh start. Oh, I pray that the eyes of your heart would be enlightened, and that the darkness of shame would be chased away. Shame keeps your eyes cast down. But God is cupping your face in His hands and calling you to look up.

Dear Lord,

I get so nervous at the thought of looking into Your eyes. I don't know if I'm ready to see myself reflected in them. I feel shame over things I've said and done, and I wonder how You could possibly forgive me. But then I look at the cross and am reminded that while I was still a sinner, You died for me [Romans 5:8]. Your love for me isn't dependent on what I do. It depends on what You have done for me. So, give me the confidence to approach Your throne of grace. I know I am promised that what I will encounter there is mercy. Always. Without exception.

DAY 21

"I will not leave you desolate." (John 14:18)

 We all need a mother. No matter how old we are, we long to be nurtured, protected, and loved. Yet many of us, for various reasons, are not receiving this tender care. We may feel like motherless daughters because our mothers have died. Or perhaps our earthly mothers weren't able or willing to love us in a way that really satisfied our needs. We might be caring for our mothers as they age, and our roles have been reversed. Whatever the reason, we can end up in a place where we're doing all we can just to hold it together. And needing to be strong all the time only intensifies the desire to find a place where we can arrive broken and needy and receive comfort.

Here's the good news: We are not orphans. We have a heavenly Father who is always there to heal, forgive, restore, and redeem us. We have a heavenly Mother who longs to spread a blanket (her mantle of protection) over us, to comfort us, to come alongside us in our times of need, to pray for us when we need strength, to help us stay on a path that leads us closer to Jesus.

Who needs Mary?

Those who don't feel known.
Those who are harsh.

Those who don't feel loved.
Those who are afraid that if they do too much, they'll be taken advantage of.
Those who are afraid of what obedience to God might cost.
Those who take care of everybody else and need someone to take care of them.
We all need a mother.

When Mary was asked to collaborate with God, she was given no guarantees—just the opportunity to love. The first thing the angel said to her was, "Do not be afraid" (Luke 1:30). Those are Mary's words to us, as well. She led by example, showing total confidence in God when she said, "Let it be to me according to your word" (Luke 1:38). She showed total confidence in Jesus when she turned to the servants at the wedding at Cana and said, "Do whatever He tells you" (John 2:5). She gives us the same message. But we hesitate, wondering how much pain or sorrow that obedience might cause us.

Mary didn't know what suffering her yes—her fiat—might bring. And we don't know, either. But we do know that we don't walk that path alone. And we know that obedience, though costly, pays eternal dividends that make any sacrifice worth it.

Dear Lord,

Thank You for the gift of Your mother.
May I follow Mary's example, uniting
my will totally to Yours. Amen.

DAY 22

"So we know and believe
the love God has for us. God
is love." (1 John 4:16)

 An appeal to the heart of God never goes unanswered. It's always met with goodness, mercy, and grace. He is so much kinder than we give Him credit for. So why do we so often behave as if God is a harsh taskmaster? The lover of our souls wants to shower us with His love, and we run in the other direction, afraid of His disapproval.

"Never enough." Does that phrase ever describe how you feel? Do you wake up and think, "I didn't get enough sleep"? Do you race through the day and crawl into bed thinking, "I didn't get enough done"? Never perfect enough. Never thin enough. Never beautiful enough. Never happy enough. Never enough.

Whose voice is this? Who whispers in your ear, "You're not enough"? Let me tell you emphatically, it is *not* God. God looks at you with kindness, and His heart fills with pride. This is the good kind of pride; it rejoices in the wonder of who you are. He says to you, "You have been given fullness in Christ! You are complete in Christ!" (Colossians 2:10).

So who is creating these expectations? Is it possible that we have heard what God desires from us and then added our own expectations and those of other people? Could it be that the feeling of being overwhelmed and inadequate is coming from trying to do things God hasn't called us to do?

When the voice whispers, "You're not enough," speak the words, "I choose love." I choose to stand under the shower of God's love and just soak it up. I choose to be measured by God's love for me—and it's unconditional, limitless, and steadfast. I choose love instead of perfection, love instead of expectations, love instead of a never-ending rat race of busyness.

We can choose to be defined by love. We can choose to love God in return by admitting that we don't have nearly as much control over things as we imagine. We can confirm our love for Him by telling Him we're glad that *He's* got it all under control. As we fill up with His love, we can ask Him to let it overflow into the lives of those around us. On our own, we're not enough. But "Christ in you, the hope of glory" (Colossians 1:27), now that's a different story.

Dear Lord,

May I choose love over perfectionism, love over comparison, love over busyness. Amen.

113

DAY 23

"Those who seek the Lord lack no good thing." (Psalm 34:10)

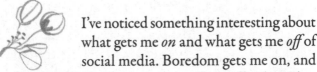

I've noticed something interesting about what gets me *on* and what gets me *off* of social media. Boredom gets me on, and I can lose track of time as I scroll mindlessly. What gets me off of social media is discontentment. I see something or someone that makes me feel bad, less than, or inadequate, so I turn it off. I think I could be spending my time a little better than this.

I'm reminded by Theodore Roosevelt that "comparison is the thief of joy." I'm tired of allowing my happiness to be robbed by something so preventable. We all know that everything presented on social media is the curated and filtered version. So why do we get caught in the trap of comparing our worst with others' best? Because who really knows what's behind that perfect picture on Facebook? Photos don't show the whole story.

Underlying our discontent is the sense that there is something better out there, and the belief that if we had it, we'd be happier. But if you look back on your life, isn't it true that as soon as you get that one thing you've been dreaming of, a new desire takes its place? The appetite for more is never satisfied.

There is a different way to live. God created you as a one-of-a-kind, creative, difference-making masterpiece. Yes, you. You are not the exception to the rule. Don't equate that description with success in your career, breathtaking Instagram feeds, or accolades. Being a world changer simply means that you take seriously the call to run *your* race without looking to the left or right and comparing yourself to others. It means trusting God that you are exactly where you are meant to be, and being faithful right there.

The baton has been passed to you, and if you refuse to run, the world will miss out on the unique gifts you have to offer.

"May you trust God that you are exactly where you are meant to be." —Saint Thérèse of Lisieux

Dear Lord,

Help me to trust that I am exactly where I am meant to be. Amen.

DAY 24

"The fear of man lays a snare, but he who trusts in the Lord is safe." (Proverbs 29:25)

 We don't always recognize fear of rejection as a personal struggle because we don't connect this fear with its fruits. This fear manifests itself as people-pleasing, approval seeking, a heightened sensitivity to criticism, feelings of worthlessness, and a rejection of others so that we can turn away before they do. We need to get to the root of this fear if we want to walk in freedom.

A snare is a trap that typically has a noose of wire or a cord. Caring too much what others think is a snare that strangles our freedom. It causes us to crave approval and fear rejection and puts people in a place meant for God alone.

We all experience rejection at some point in our lives. It's unavoidable. But being afraid of it or totally train-wrecked by it is optional. It all boils down to what our identity is based on. If the way our worth is defined is through people's acceptance of us, then fear of rejection will always be a noose around our necks. But if we can totally embrace the truth that people's opinions do not determine our worth or identity, that our worth is determined by God and our identity is rooted in being His beloved daughters, then freedom can be ours.

God's approval is the only one that ultimately matters, and He *adores you*. Yes, *you*. You are not an exception to the rule, no matter what you've done or what you're struggling with today.

Do you want to see God show up in your life in a powerful way? Are you tired of the status quo and ready for more? Would you like to see God, in all His glory, intersect your circumstances?

God wants us to experience His glory. He wants to pour out His power on us and see us living freed, transformed lives. This has always been His desire. When Jesus walked the earth, there was nothing He wanted more than for the people to see His glory and to be changed as a result. But so many of them missed it. Why? The reason is found in the Gospel of John: "for they loved the praise of men more than the praise of God" (John 12:43). They wanted something more than God's power and glory. They wanted human praise. Jesus is turning to you now and asking, "What do you want?" How will you answer Him?

Dear Lord,

Help me to care more about what You think of me than what anyone else thinks. Amen.

DAY 25

"But the woman, knowing what had been done to her, came in fear and trembling and fell down before him, and told him the whole truth." (Mark 5:33)

 In a pressing crowd, there was a woman who had been hemorrhaging for years. She believed that if she could just touch Jesus' cloak, she would be healed. She moved forward, reached out, and touched His garment, and Jesus felt it. He felt the touch of her faith. Immediately He began to look for her, asking, "Who touched me?" The disciples must have thought He was crazy. All sorts of people were touching Him—that was the nature of being in a crowd of people. But Jesus was looking among the crowd for one specific woman who needed to tell the truth.

The woman's bleeding had stopped when she touched Jesus, but there was a deeper healing He wanted to give her. This would require her telling Him the whole truth. She did and was fully healed as a result.

Jesus asks the same of us. If we are afraid to tell the whole truth and instead hide, our healing will remain out of reach. When we develop a pattern of insisting that everything in our lives is fine when it isn't, of avoiding conflict, of smiling when our hearts are breaking, we can become such good liars that we don't even realize we aren't telling the truth. When we ignore huge parts of our stories, we are betraying ourselves. We are living a lie that keeps us in bondage and far from freedom.

Your truth needs to be spoken. Burying it under coping mechanisms and peacekeeping compromises weakens the muscle you need to have strong for those times in life when your *yes* or *no* really matters. If you are able to say *no* to your spouse or your parent or your boss in the little things, then one day when your *no* has far bigger consequences, you'll be able to do it.

Telling the whole truth builds our character. Stuffing our emotions, lying about how we really are, weakens it. When a crisis hits, our true character will be revealed. If our character is strong, we will be likely to learn something through suffering. If our character is weak, we'll be apt to blame others and think the world (or God) is unfair.

Telling the whole truth is critical if we want to be well and strong. Bring it all to God. Hold nothing back. He can handle it.

Dear Lord,

I am grateful that nothing shocks You.
Help me to speak my truth to You and
others that I may be healed. Amen.

DAY
26

"A broken and contrite heart, O God, you will not despise." (Psalm 51:17)

One lesson that I've learned over the past decade is that what we offer to the Lord does not need to be perfect in order to be good. In fact, when we are weak and imperfect, that is when He shows up most powerfully.

In *hindsight*, it has been during times of brokenness that I have most fully seen God's goodness and blessing being extended to me. But in the *middle* of it, I don't. When we're stuck in the middle, we are susceptible to lies about the heart of the Father. We question His love, His goodness, His power, and His interest in us.

In his book *Life of the Beloved*, Henri Nouwen writes about the importance of putting our brokenness under the blessing. All too often, what we do instead is put our brokenness under the curse. We do this when we allow our difficult circumstances to confirm lies that have been swirling in our heads. We filter our current experience through the lies, and it feels true.

We are called to resist this train of thought, to see it for what it is—a road to hopelessness. Instead, we bring our brokenness and stand under the blessing of God's grace. We are honest with Him in terms of how we feel, but we speak truth about what we know of His character.

God's desire is for us to accept ourselves as His beloved in the very moments when we feel least deserving of it. I'm moved by John Steinbeck's words, "And now that you don't have to be perfect, you can be good." When we can rest in God's grace, when our belovedness doesn't feel like it is perpetually on the line, we are free to love. Recognizing that God loves us in our brokenness frees us from the chains of perfectionism and allows us to extend that same grace to others. We can invite our loved ones to exhale and drop the mask. We can become soft places for others' hearts to land because we aren't so busy trying to prove ourselves. The unconditional love we have received is passed on to people who are desperate for a place to belong and call home.

Dear Lord,

Thank You for welcoming me as I am. Not the cleaned-up version of me, but the real me. In my weakness, in my brokenness, You still call me beloved. Thank You for loving me in this way. Amen.

DAY 27

"I will turn the darkness before them into light, the rough places into level ground." (Isaiah 42:16)

God invites you to step out and trust Him in the scary places. He may be inviting you to stop trying to control someone in your life and instead to trust Him to intervene. Perhaps it's a hard conversation He wants you to have. Maybe it's finally working up the courage to say out loud, "I am drinking to numb the pain and I don't know how to stop." It could be that He's asking you to admit that you are experiencing despair, and that you need professional help. It's a stepping out into the unknown, and even as He extends His hand, the pretend places of safety look preferable to the free fall of trust.

And that's where God meets us. When we quit pretending, when we stop burying the things that need attention, He stands right in front of us, cups our face in His hands, and whispers, "You are so brave."

He cheers when we take that first, scary step. He knows that's the hardest step to take. He calls to our hearts, "Fear not, for I have redeemed you; I have summoned you by name; you are mine!" (Isaiah 43:1). He grabs hold of our hands and does not let go for one second. His strength is infused into us, and we find that we can take another step, and then the next. Every single moment of the free fall, He goes before us, turning the darkness into light and making the rough places smooth. He coaxes us forward and promises, "When you pass through the waters, I will be with you. When you pass through the rivers, they will not sweep over you. When you walk through the fire, you will not be burned; the flames will not set you ablaze" (Isaiah 43:2).

Ask the One who loves you to give you just a little more courage than fear. That's all you need to take the first step. You don't need to have it all scripted out. You don't need to have the whole plan in place. You just need a little more courage than fear, and the knowledge of where the free fall ends. Oh, my sweet friend, it doesn't end with you in a heap on the floor. It ends with you cradled in His arms. You can rest there. And when the time is right, He'll set your feet back on the ground and say, "See, I am doing a new thing! Now it springs up; do you not perceive it? I am making a way in the desert and streams in the wasteland" (Isaiah 43:18–19).

Dear Lord,

I am grateful for Your mercy
that never fails. Amen.

DAY 28

"Let me hear in the morning of your merciful love, for in you I put my trust. Teach me the way I should go, for to you I lift up my soul." (Psalms 143:8)

What are your first thoughts when you wake up? Does the to-do list start to run in your head before your feet hit the floor? Does regret weigh your heart before you've had your coffee? Does anxiety have you in its grip before you can pray?

We can't help the thoughts and emotions we wake with, but we can decide what we are going to focus on as we move forward. Instead of letting what we feel take charge, we can choose to focus on truth.

Do you know that God sings over you? Zephaniah 3:17 says, "The Lord, your God, is in your midst, a warrior who gives victory; he will rejoice over you with gladness, he will renew you in his love; he will exult over you with loud singing." Each morning that you wake up to a life that feels like a battle, God wants to remind you that He is a warrior who gives victory. He sees all that you face and promises to fight alongside you, in front of you, within you, and behind you. Victory is guaranteed because He is a mighty warrior.

As God fights by your side, He rejoices over you with gladness and sings. Why? Because you bring Him so much joy. He does not look at you with eyes of disappointment. He is not there telling you to pull yourself up by your bootstraps (an impossible task, at any rate). He is there, delighting in you.

His delight is not based on what you accomplish, what you look like, or what others think of you. He delights in you simply because you belong to Him. You are His child.

He waits every morning to see if you will turn to Him in trust and lift up your soul. Is your soul weary? He will fill you with strength. Is your soul battered? He will heal your wounds. Is your soul feeling abandoned? He will embrace you.

There is no one more worthy of your trust than the Lord. He will never leave you or forsake you. He truly understands what you face. He knows what will get you through the trials. Ask Him to teach you in the way that you should go, and He will faithfully lead you.

Dear Lord,

May I turn my face to Your merciful love before I do anything else in my day. I trust You. I lift my soul to You. Teach me the way I should go. Amen.

DAY 29

"Man, tempted by the devil, let his trust in his Creator die in his heart and, abusing his freedom, disobeyed God's command. This is what man's first sin consisted of. All subsequent sin would be disobedience toward God and lack of trust in his goodness." (CCC 397)

 What virtue could have protected Eve from all the trouble she got into? It's the same virtue that can keep us from despair, or from taking matters into our own hands. It's the virtue of trust. Underneath Eve's discontentment and susceptibility to temptation was a lack of trust in God. Did He really want the best for her, or was He holding back? Was His way truly the one that would lead to freedom and fulfillment? Was He worthy of trust?

Have you ever been in a situation of real need, only to discover that the friend you thought you could count on was nowhere to be found? While you may have continued with the friendship, no doubt your trust in that person was eroded. We trust those who are with us and for us, who we know will stay by our side in the hard times.

Trust in Christ is never misplaced. He proved to us that He is in it for the long haul, *for our sake*, when He suffered and hung on the cross. He could have taken the easy way out, but He didn't. He stayed on the cross for *you*.

In the times when people might desert us, that is when He is nearest. It's a comfort to know that He hears each spoken need. Every detail of our life matters to Him. He cares. We don't always perceive His work, but He always acts on our behalf.

When life seems too much and disappointments weigh heavily on our hearts, when the future seems scary, God invites us to trust Him enough to hide in Him. He encourages us to shed the masks that conceal our true selves, crawl into His lap, and let Him shelter us in His love.

Don't make Eve's mistake. Don't forget who you are. You are God's beloved daughter. He gave everything so that you could have that privilege. The intimacy that Eve lost in the garden is available to you. God calls to His tired, weak, and wandering daughters, "Come home and rest in my love! Your strength will return as you rest in me. I call you by name. You are mine. All you long for can be found in me. I am worthy of your trust. Hide yourself in my love."

Dear Lord,

I am tired and weary. The effort it takes to shield myself is exhausting me. I am ready to hand over the reins to You. Jesus, I trust in You. Take care of everything. Amen.

"But Martha was distracted with much serving; and she went to him and said, 'Lord, do you not care that my sister has left me to serve alone? Tell her then to help me.'" (Luke 10:40)

Martha asked, "Lord, do you not care?" Mary's unwillingness to help seemed like such a selfish choice. The injustice appeared obvious. When Jesus responded by defending Mary's choice, Martha must have been taken aback. No matter how gently He said it, exhausted Martha must have been incredulous that somehow she was the one being criticized.

Jesus' reason for siding with Mary wasn't because He didn't care about Martha; He pointed to a different choice precisely because He cared about Martha *so much*. It was clear to Jesus that she defined her worth by her productivity. Every time her burst of energy and hard work resulted in a successful event or a sense of accomplishment, she felt like she mattered. She measured her worth by her performance.

Jesus was inviting Martha to sit at His feet, because that is the best place to learn *who* we really are. When we are in productivity mode, we remember what we can *do*. Those are two very different things.

We produce a lot and then we're likely to fall into the traps of self-sufficiency and pride. Or we don't produce enough and we feel like failures. Both responses leave us vulnerable to believing the wrong messages about who we are and what we're worth.

The world is constantly sending us messages about who we are. "You are what you produce." "You are what you eat." "You are what you wear." "You are what you make of yourself." Jesus invites us to sit at His feet and fill up our minds with His perspective. Sit at His feet and remember who you really are.

Dear Lord,

Help me to remember that You love me because I belong to You, not because I'm perfect or because of the things I do. Give me the mind of Christ so that I will live out the truth that I cannot earn Your love; it is unconditional. Help me to lift my eyes to Your face and see reflected back all the warmth, compassion, mercy, and grace that radiates from Your heart. Who am I? I am Your beloved daughter. When I fail, You fill in the gaps. When I see all I lack, You remind me that You, within me, are enough. When I'm tempted to beat myself up, You remind me that You took the beating so that I could rest in grace. Help me to do that. May I cease my striving, because my worth was defined and settled when You died for me on the cross. Amen.

DAY 31

"For our sake he made him to be sin who knew no sin, so that in him we might become the righteousness of God." (2 Corinthians 5:21)

How did God make Him who had no sin to be sin for you? This was foretold by the prophet Isaiah: "But he was wounded for our transgressions, he was bruised for our iniquities; upon him was the chastisement that made us whole, and with his stripes we are healed" (Isaiah 53:5).

Jesus accomplished this on the cross. Every sin committed, past, present, and future, was placed on Him. Now *all the merits of Jesus can be yours.* He wants to fill your empty hands with His own virtues.

But first you need to recognize, just as Saint Thérèse of Lisieux did, that you are little. You are weak. You fail. You need forgiveness. You need a savior. When you come before God in prayer and acknowledge these truths, He looks at your heart. He sees your desire to trust Him, to please Him, to obey Him. He says to you, "My precious child, you don't have to pay for your sins. My Son, Jesus, has already done that for you. He suffered so that you wouldn't have to. I want to experience a relationship of intimacy with you. I forgive you. Jesus came to set you free. When you open your heart to Me, you become a new creation! The old you has gone. The new you is here.

If you will stay close to Me, and journey by My side, you will begin to experience a transformation that brings joy and freedom. I've been waiting to pour My gifts into your soul. Beloved daughter of Mine, remain confident in Me. I am your loving Father. Crawl into My lap. Trust Me. Love Me. I will take care of everything."

This is conversion of heart. This act of faith lifts the veil from your eyes and launches you into the richest and most satisfying life. You don't have to be sitting in church to do this. Don't let a minute pass before opening your heart to God and inviting Him to come dwell within you. Let Him sit in the driver's seat. Give Him the keys to your heart. Your life will never be the same again.

Dear Lord,

I need a savior. I've tried to do it all on my own, and that hasn't gone so well. I want to invite You to be the One in charge. I give You my heart. I offer You the keys and invite You to come in and fill me. Amen.

1   Matt Nelson, *Just Whatever: How to Help the Spiritually Indifferent Find Beliefs That Really Matter* (El Cajon, CA: Catholic Answers, 2018), 64.

2   "Millennials at Church," Barna, March 4, 2015, https://www.barna.com/research/what-millennials-want-when-they-visit-church/.

3   Christopher West, *Our Bodies Tell God's Story* (Grand Rapids, MI: Baker Publishing Group, 2020), 89.

4   William Barclay, *The Gospel of John, Vol. 1* (Louisville, KY: Westminster John Knox Press, 2017), 176.

5   Emily Nagoski and Amelia Nagoski, *Burnout: The Secret to Unlocking the Stress Cycle* (New York: Ballantine Books, 2020), 190.

6   Tim Keller, "The Rest Giver," Christ Our Treasure: The Book of Hebrews (sermon series, Redeemer Presbyterian Church, New York City, February 20, 2005).

7   "Aleksander Solzhenitsyn, The Gulag Archipelago," Quotes.net, https://www.quotes.net/authors/Aleksander+Solzhenitsyn%2C+The+Gulag+Archipelago.

8   Father Dave Pivonka and 4PM Media, "Sin and Mercy," *Metanoia* (video series), Wild Goose Ministries, https://wildgoose.tv/programs/4-sin-and-mercy?categoryId=23146.

9   "Goodness, Truth, and Beauty," Catholic Quotations, https://catholicquotations.com/truth-and-beauty/.

10 George MacDonald, "Abba Father," The Literature Network, http://www.online-literature.com/george-macdonald/3669/.

11 "The Father Revealed by the Son," 239, *The Catechism of the Catholic Church*, 2nd ed. (Rome: Libreria Editrice Vaticana, 2012).

12 W. Phillip Keller, *A Shepherd Looks at Psalm 23* (Grand Rapids, MI: Zondervan, 2007), 60.

13 Nancy Guthrie, "Can I Really Expect God to Protect Me?" *Christianity Today*, October 10, 2005, https://www.christianitytoday.com/ct/2005/october/26.56.html.

14 Guthrie, "Can I Really Expect God to Protect Me?"

15 Guthrie, "Can I Really Expect God to Protect Me?"

16 Guthrie, "Can I Really Expect God to Protect Me?"

17 Father John Bartunek, *The Better Part* (Hamden, CT: Circle Press, 2007), 819.

18 Linda Dillow, *Calm My Anxious Heart: A Woman's Guide to Finding Contentment* (Colorado Springs: NavPress, 1998), 120.

19 Sarah Young, *Jesus Calling: Enjoying Peace in His Presence* (Nashville, TN: Thomas Nelson, 2004), 304.

20 Richard Winter, "Perfectionism: The Road to Heaven—or Hell?" L'Abri Papers No. RW01, http://www.labri.org/england/resources/05052008/RW01_Perfectionism.pdf.

21 "Millennials at Church," Barna, March 4, 2015, https://www.barna.com/research/what-millennials-want-when-they-visit-church/.

22 "Millennials at Church", March 4, 2015, https://www.barna.com/research/what-millennials-want-when-they-visit-church/, accessed April 17, 2020.

Continue with daily reflections in God's love story, Be Still...

A Daily Devotional to Quiet Your Heart

What does it mean to live the good life?
How can you be happy?
What choices will get you there?

Grow closer to the Lord every day with *Be Still*, the 365-day devotional from Walking with Purpose. This beautifully designed hardcover devotional collection will renew your mind by helping you look at things from God's perspective, day by day.

Each of the readings in *Be Still* begin with a Bible verse, followed by a reflection on how we can apply it to our daily lives, and a short prayer. The writings aim to touch the heart, strengthen the will, and enlighten the mind. If you apply what you read, you will make significant progress in the spiritual life!

Learn more about *Be Still* at shop.walkingwithpurpose.com

walking with purpose

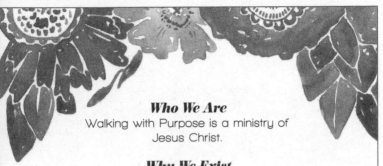

Who We Are
Walking with Purpose is a ministry of
Jesus Christ.

Why We Exist
We exist to enable women to know Jesus Christ
personally through Scripture and the teachings of the
Roman Catholic Church.

Our Mission
Our mission is to help every Catholic woman and girl in
America to open her heart to Jesus Christ.

Our Vision
Our vision for the future is that, as more Catholic women
deepen their relationships with Jesus Christ, eternity-
changing transformation will take place in their hearts –
and, by extension – in their families, in their communities,
and ultimately, in our nation.

walking with purpose

You can support our mission through a tax-deductible gift.
Learn more at walkingwithpurpose.com/donate